# A Sense of Direction

# A Sense of Direction

## of Direction

*Some Observations on the Art of Directing*

# William Ball

DRAMA BOOK PUBLISHERS *New York*

Copyright © 1984 by William Ball
First Edition
All rights reserved under the International and Pan-American
Copyright Conventions. For information address
Drama Book Publishers, 821 Broadway, New York, New York 10003
or author's agent, Marian Searchinger Associates,
327 Central Park West, New York, New York 10027.

Library of Congress Cataloguing in Publication Data
Ball, William, 1931-
   *A sense of direction.*
   1. Theater—Production and direction.   2. Acting.
I. Title.
PN2053.B313   1984      792'.0233      84-8104

ISBN 0-89676-081-2
ISBN 0-89676-082-0 (pbk.)

Text design by Angelica Design Group, New York City
Printed and bound in the United States of America

90  89  88  87  86  85       0  9  8  7  6  5  4  3  2

# Dedication

This book is dedicated to the well-being of actors and in particular to those with whom I have worked at A.C.T., among whom

Linda Aldrich
Hugh Alexander
Wayne Alexander
Hope Alexander-Willis
Jeffrey Allin
Al Alu
Janie Atkins
Rene Auberjonois, R.A.A.
Len Auclair
Andy Backer
Jim Baker
Eugene Barcone
Candace Barrett
Barbara Barrie
Annette Bening
Martin Berman
Ramon Bieri
Joseph Bird
Raye Birk
Scot Bishop
Roberts Blossom
Earl Boen
Libby Boone
Ronald Boussom
Bonnie Bowers
Bonita Bradley
Mark Bramhall
Peter Bretz
John Brown
Lauren Brown
R. Aaron Brown
Roscoe Lee Browne
James L. Burke
Marty Burke
Michael Burnor

Emilya Cachapero
Karie Cannon
Joy Carlin
Nancy Carlin
Larry Carpenter
Mimi Carr
Richard Carreon
Michelle Casey
Michael Cavanaugh
Jeffrey Chandler
Ludi Claire
Barbara Colby
Megan Cole
Suzanne Collins
Nicholas Cortland
Jacqueline Coslow
Richard Council
Penelope Court
Kathryn Crosby
Joan Croydon
David Cryer
Joan Darling
Peter Davies
Daniel Davis
Heidi Helen Davis
George Deloy
John De Mita
Richard Denison
Barbara Dirickson
Peter Donat, R.A.A.
Franchelle Dorn
William Douglas
Jay Doyle
Jeff Druce
David Dukes

Richard A. Dysart
Rick Echols
George Ede
James Edmondson
Dana Elcar
Bobby Ellerbee
Geoffrey Elliott
Sabin Epstein
Drew Eshelman
Donald Ewer
Patricia Falkenhaim
Gina Ferrall
Ed Flanders
John Fletcher
Julia Fletcher
Robert Fletcher
Melvin Flood
Lois Foraker
Herbert Foster
Harry Frazier
Scott Freeman
Dorothy French
Ralph Funicello
June Gable
Robin Gammell
Mary Garrett
Ellen Geer
Will Geer
Fred Geick, C.A.A.
Lynn George
Robert Gerringer
Ann Gillespie
David Gilliam
Jerry Glover
Patrick Gorman

*v*

Linda Graham
Sarina Grant
Wendell Grayson
Robert Ground
Bennett Guillory
James Haire
Charles Hallahan
Rick Hamilton
Harry Hamlin
John Hancock
Lydia Hannibal
Mark Harelik
Katheleen Harper
Thomas Harrison
Edward Hasting
Helaine Head
Lawrence Hecht
John Noah Hertzler
Leslie Hicks
Jill Hill
Scott Hitchcock
Henry Hoffman
Nancy Houfek
Elizabeth Huddle
David Hudson
Peggy Hughes
Michael Hume
David Hurst
Janice Hutchins
John Hutton
Scott Hylands
Charles Hyman
Amy Ingersoll
Gregory Itzen
Johanna Jackson
Nagle Jackson
Carol Mayo Jenkins
Byron Jennings
Jane Jones
Nicholas Kaledin
Enid Kent
Daniel Kern
Roger Kern
Phillip Kerr
Jim Kershaw
Michael Keys-Hall
Randall Duk Kim
Laura Klein

Judith Knaiz
Ruth Kobart
Barry Kraft
Wortham Krimmer
Gerald Lancaster
Robert Lanchester
Charles Lanyer
Dana Larson
Anne Lawder
Michael Learned, R.A.A.
Michael Lerner
Laurence Luckinbill
Claire Malis
Winifred Mann
David Margulies
Douglas Martin
Michael X. Martin
Marsha Mason, R.A.A.
Dakin Matthews
George Mauricio
Deborah May
Glenn Mazen
Jeff McCarthy
Carolyn McCormick
Nancy Mcdoniel
Matt McKenzie
William McKereghan
Anne McNaughton
Meribeth Meachem
De Ann Mears, R.A.A.
Kirsten Mickelwait
Judith Mihalyi
James Milton
Delores Mitchell
Ed Mock
William Molloy
Robert Mooney
Tom Moore
Judith Moreland
Mark Murphey
Thomas Nahrwold
Alex Nibley
Josephine Nichols
Tom O'Brien
Thomas Oglesby
Michael O'Guinne
Fredi Olster
Michael O'Sullivan

Frank Ottiwell
William Paterson, R.A.A.
Greg Patterson
Angela Paton
Austin Pendleton
Susan Pellegrino
Jane Percival
Rick Poe
Charlene Polite
Herman Poppe
Dennis Powers
Jim Poyner
E. Kerrigan Prescott
Jane Preston
Dianne Prichard
Kathleen Quirin
Ellis Rabb, C.A.A.
Wendi Radford
Stacy Ray
Ray Reinhardt, R.A.A.
Pat Rice
Randall Richard
Eve Roberts
Jeremy Roberts
Joel Rudnick
Ken Ruta
Jay Sanders
Frank Savino
Mark Schell
Stephen Schnetzer
John Schuck
Donovan Scott
Richard Seger
Paul Shenar, R.A.A.
Howard Sherman
Warner Shook
Charles Seibert
Cynthia Sikes
Garland Simpson
Robert Simpson
Marc Singer
Shirley Slater
Alice Smith
Anna Deavere Smith
Bo Smith
Randall Smith
Rosemary Smith
Sally Smythe

Donna Snow
Josef Sommer
Theodore Sorel
Guy Spaull
Beulah Steen
James Stephens
Harold Surratt
Deborah Sussel
Francine Tacker
Tom V. V. Tammi
Bonnie Tarwater
Alec Teague
Carol Teitel
Angela Thieriot
Scott Thomas

Tynia Thomassie
Sada Thompson, R.A.A.
Patrick Tovatt
Patrick Treadway
Cicely Tyson, R.A.A.
Karen Van Zandt
Sydney Walker, R.A.A.
Lee Wallace
Marrian Walters, R.A.A.
Denzel Washington
Marshall Watson
Ann Weldon
Robert Westenberg
Mark Wheeler
Al White

J. Steven White
Mary Wickes
Nancy Wickwire
John Wilk
Bruce Williams
Laird Williamson
James Winker
Michael Winters
Isiah Whitlock, Jr.
G. Wood
Laura Ann Worthen
D. Paul Yeuell
Daniel Zippi
. . . and many others

# Contents

## Connotations  150

## An Epilogue  175

## Appendix  179

## Biographical Note  181

# Preface

When the great stage director Sir Tyrone Guthrie used to speak to students he referred to his lectures as "pie-jaw." In his native Ireland "pie-jaw" was the expression given to the "good advice" that grandmothers used to give to children. In a manner of speaking, this little book is a bit of "pie-jaw."

Although I usually avoid the invitation to give advice, these chapters are composed of some common-sense techniques for young stage directors. The book had its genesis in a series of lectures on directing that I gave at the American Conservatory Theatre in San Francisco. I have allowed myself great latitude in the style of presentation—now and then including the young directors' questions in the text, occasionally addressing the students directly in the second person, and permitting myself to meander off into personal reminiscences and little stories to provide examples.

The material in this book is divided into two sections. The first section is devoted to the principles that influence the director's primary decisions. The second section deals with the practical do's and don't's of stage direction—the specific techniques of our work. I suggest that the impatient reader jump right in and begin with chapter 4. But for the reader with more time, the first three chapters include reflections on some of the theories that serve as the underpinning of the director's purpose.

My motive in putting this material into written form was threefold. For one thing, there seems to be a concern in the American theatre about the emergence of skilled directors. "Where are all the young directors to come from? Who will carry on the great legacy of Guthrie, Brook, Kazan, and Nichols?"

Secondly, I have received an increasing number of questionnaires and requests for interviews from university teachers and students asking, "How do you work?"

My third reason for jotting down these impressions on directorial technique is that most of the members of our A.C.T. company have, at one time or another, been asked to direct new plays or student projects. By putting all my answers in one place, I hope to satisfy the odd assortment of questions that have dotted our conversations through the many seasons of our creative work together.

I have used a very informal approach in this book, in part to preserve the spirit of personal talks with the students. Directing is not an exact science and does not lend itself easily to academic textbook treatment. Indeed most of the texts devoted to techniques of directing strike me as bloodless and impractical. I harbor a faint hope that somewhere within these pages the young theatre lover may come upon a sentence, a phrase, a word that may unexpectedly crack the great dark crust and let in a thread of light—a moment of illumination that will make things clearer.

I would like to acknowledge the influence of my teachers, Allen Fletcher, C.A.A., and Henry Boettcher; the support of W. McNeil Lowry, James B. McKenzie, C.A.A., and Benjamin Moore; the aid of Marne and Peter Kellogg; the kindness and encouragement of Peggy Hughes, Penny Simi, Doug Martin, Scot Bishop, and especially Kay Craig.

# A Sense of Direction

*Pay no attention to that man
behind the curtain.*

THE WIZARD OF OZ

# Art, Consciousness, Belief, Unity

## ART

My particular prejudice is that the theatre is an art form, and everything that I have to say to you will relate to theatre as an art. When speaking of art, we can make some generalizations that do not pertain to, let us say, business or industry.

The most important characteristic of a work of art is unity. The one thing that every work of art has at its center is unity. If it lacks unity, it does not qualify as a work of art. Unity means harmony among the component parts; and the greater the harmony among the component parts, the greater the unity and the greater the art. What we seek are techniques that will increase the harmony among the component parts.

The second characteristic of a work of art is that it reveals Universe. Show business does not have to reveal Universe. It is not required and not expected. Night club entertainment is not expected to reveal Universe. Vaudeville is not expected to reveal Universe. Theatre or drama is expected to reveal Universe.

A third thing that art does is awaken the Spirit. Commerce is not expected to awaken Spirit and neither is show business. By awakening the Spirit, we mean that somewhere during the course of the performance, the spectator experiences "The Great Aha!" A light goes on within him and the self is illuminated, awakened, enlightened, elevated, and changed. Usually the moment of awakening is very short, and it is an unconscious moment. One is sometimes aware that it took place *after* it has happened, but while it is happening, one is unaware.

There is something else that the work of art in the theatre is expected to have that show business and television entertainment are not necessarily expected to have. That has to do with the revelation of the beauty of humankind. That beauty, concealed somewhere within the drama, takes many forms, and the revelation takes many forms, but one may witness and share the author's vision—his admiration, awe, and wonder at that beauty—through a work of art. When it is not art, it lacks a sense of the beauty of humankind. These are generalizations, but I do want to separate the discussion of art from show business and entertainment so that no one is misled.

Shall we start right off by talking about how to block a play? Shall we begin with the connotative value of colors? Shall we say how to handle a difficult actor? As we begin to talk about theatre as art, how deeply shall we go? To a discussion of the nature of art? Yes, but let's go deeper than that. Shall we go, for instance, to the relation of art to humanity? Yes, but let's go deeper than that. Let's go deeper than the word "art." Let's find out where art comes from. I want to begin at the source. Let's go as close to the center of experience as we can.

## CONSCIOUSNESS

Consciousness is the beginning of what we consider awareness. Let's start with consciousness and go from consciousness upward to the level of plays. A play in a theatre is a peculiar convention. It is more than peculiar. It's absurd, it's ungainly, it's awkward, it's unbelievable, it's inexplicable. In our society, as busy and playful as it is, a thousand people walk up to a little window and pay for the privilege of going into a dark room and sitting there for three hours while a group of people at the other end of the dark room impersonate human behavior. At the conclusion of this process, the thousand people who have been sitting silently and motionlessly in the dark clap their hands, signifying satisfaction, and return to their regular lives. It is a peculiar activity, especially when you consider that human beings do not usually sit together in the dark for three hours motionlessly and silently giving their undivided attention to something outside themselves. Human beings like to give attention to their *needs*. To sit in silence and give their attention to something outside of themselves is a very rare experience.

Metaphysics is the center of all experience. That man who does not live in awe of something outside himself is dead. The experience of drama is one of those moments in which a human being sits in awe, wonder, and admiration of something outside of self.

The experience of consciousness is the awareness of self. The first human experience is "I am." Consciousness is the beginning. "I am" is the beginning. Now, after consciousness comes identity. When a word is placed after "I am," universal consciousness becomes individuated. Absolute becomes focused as relative. "I am a director." Suddenly my consciousness is limited and defined. An individual may have six or eight overlapping identities. "I am husband, I am father, I am broker, I am Republican, I am Presbyterian, I am golfer, I am magazine subscriber, I am diabetic, I am stamp collector." The individual's belief in his identities gives a pattern to his reality and a definition to his activity. He limits his beliefs in order to maintain identities that are manageable, comfy, respectable.

Now, the actor commits himself to a lifetime of beliefs in an endless series of identities. The actor spends his professional life completing the phrase "I am"; and every time he plays a different part, he completes that phrase differently. "I am butcher, I am banker, I am president, I am drunkard, I am lover, I am king, I am villain, I am daughter, I am gardener." An actor is perpetually combining the primary statement of consciousness with identity, and that identity is constantly changing. The actor has an empty space after the phrase "I am"; the actor says, "I am anyone and I am everyone." That's what makes an actor different from a broker.

The actor makes a profession of believing in many identities. Ask an actor if he would limit his potential identities or limit his power of belief. No. An actor claims the unlimited power of belief. He claims the right to unlimited identities. He considers that the very definition of his profession guarantees his right to an unlimited power of belief. "I am anyone, I am everyone, I am all, I am Universe." The actor claims the right of universal dominion.

This puts the actor in an extraordinary position—his work is centered in consciousness, identity, and belief. Power. This is his vision.

The actor sees himself as potential Universe. He is revealer of Universe. He is demonstrator of Universe. The actor is claiming unlimited power to believe himself in every identity. "I am anyone, everyone, anything, everything, and essentially all, or Universe." He may have holes in his socks, but he claims unlimited power of belief; that is, he claims that he is Universe walking in body. The awareness that he is talking to a person who is the demonstration of Universe revealing will change the way a director talks to an actor. There is no power on earth that can shake the actor's belief that he is, in fact, Universe revealing; but he never says it out loud. People would call him crazy. He doesn't brag about it, he doesn't fight about it, and he certainly doesn't articulate it, because he knows that a man who wears a top hat gets a brick thrown at it. The artist is conscious of a vision of the Universe; the condition of his socks is only material. We are now talking about the consciousness of the artist as opposed to the consciousness of a showman, or a performer.

That consciousness may make an actor seem to be vague when you have a conversation with him. He may seem detached, shy, uncommitted, because at that moment he is not "driving the car." He is not doing his thing. He is "in between." When you talk to them, most actors have a peculiar quality of incompleteness, a kind of uncertainty or vagueness. The reason for this is that they are waiting to assume identity. As a director, you have to be aware that your actor is superhuman in one aspect, and that the likelihood is that he will be vague or dull in another aspect. His behavior may be vague, but his power is limitless. As a director dealing with this peculiar combination, you have to regard his power as sacred and approach it with all gentleness, with great respect. On the other hand, you understand that when an actor is not firm in his identity, he needs support and strength, instruction and guidance. While he is living outside of his chosen identity, he seems to have a perpetual sense of sublime bafflement. The director is entrusted with the care of these very special creatures. They are unique in society, and most of society does not understand them.

We have established that consciousness of Universe is the beginning place for actors; that the actor believes he contains universal light; and that his entire life is devoted to revealing his vision of Universe as clearly and as resplendently as possible. An actor's great longing is to be witnessed. He believes his vision of life to be unique and magnificent. He believes that his vision is a solo vision and that no one has quite the same magnificent vision. He feels a sense of urgency that his vision reach the world. He feels that the world will be less splendid until his vision enhances it. The actor feels compelled to bring light or illumination into life; he is a purveyor of light. The actor's big question is: "Where is the on-switch?" And the director, by helping the actor find the switch, gives the actor the one thing he wants—the power to bring light into the darkened room.

## BELIEF

It has been said that belief is more powerful than knowledge. We've heard expressions like "Faith moves mountains" or "Where medicine could not cure him, his belief cured him." We've heard of people making tremendous sacrifices for their beliefs.

Belief is a different "apparatus" than knowledge. In our times, belief is more powerful than knowledge. What you believe you are is what you are. If you believe yourself to be weak, you are weak. If you believe yourself to be a success, you are a success. If you believe that you will have trouble, you will have trouble. If you believe that you will be rich, you will be rich. If you believe that there is no hope, there is no hope. All human activity is based on belief. Knowledge affects human events, but belief causes them.

A painter builds with color and line; a musician with tone and rhythm. A sculptor builds with shape. But the actor builds his profession on patterns of belief. An actor is working with the same tool that causes all events. That is belief. Belief is the power that causes things to happen, and actors are exercising their belief power all the time. If one says to an actor, "Will you please believe this?" he will do so readily. It is difficult for him to resist the tendency to become whatever is suggested. The actor rises to the occasion automatically. He quickly enters into almost any situation and believes in almost any suggestion just as a child does. That belief power has tremendous force. We say that in the theatre we "make believe," just as children make believe. What belief do we "make"? The actor makes himself believe. Then he makes the audience believe. The actor believes in himself, in his character, and in his work. The audience believes in the characters, in the story, and in the players.

There is a great deal of belief going on around a theatre during a performance. Belief power is pervasive in a theatre, and belief power is tremendously compelling. This is one of the reasons that audiences will sit in the darkness giving their undivided attention to individuals who believe themselves to be other than who they are. The belief on the stage is so compelling that the audience starts to believe these individuals *are* who they say they are. When an audience believes and the actors believe, we have a tremendous concentration of energy. It is spellbinding. The more the audience believes what the actor is doing, the more the actor will believe what he is doing. And the more the actor believes what he is doing, the more the audience will believe. It's a self-hypnosis of belief. It's a rapture of belief. It's an orgy of belief. When the play is over, we return to our customary identities. The broker has been believing himself to be in real trouble; believing himself to be wrapped in love; believing himself to be in danger; believing himself to be in triumph, and on and on. When the final curtain falls, he returns to the belief that he is a husband, a golfer, a Republican, a father. He has come to the theatre to "exercise" his *systems of belief*. The more exercise or stimulation his belief systems get, the more exhilaration and pleasure he receives. When he leaves the theatre, he may say, "That was a wonderful show! That was a great play! That was really absorbing!" The reason his spirit is so renewed and enthusiastic is that his belief systems have been awakened and exhilarated. During the course of the performance he contributed so much of his belief that new aspects of his identity have been awakened.

## UNITY

When all of the actors believe in what they are doing and all members of the audience believe in what they are witnessing, we have all component parts believing something at the same time. The actors believe one another, each actor believes himself, each spectator believes each actor, everyone is believing at the same time. All component parts are in harmony. When all component parts are in harmony, we have the possibility of a work of art—we have unity.

I'd like to draw attention to the last seven minutes before a play comes to an end. Seven minutes is an arbitrary length of time, but we will use it to represent an experience that frequently occurs a few minutes before the final curtain. Actually, it is not the last seven minutes; it is the last seven minutes before the last three minutes. Let's work up to this from the beginning.

The curtain rises: For the first ten minutes, the audience is curious, distracted, detached, and even skeptical. "You can't draw me in. I know the scenery is fake, I know the language is artificial, I know I am holding a program, I know I may have to fight for control of the arm rest, I know I just had dinner, I know my objective reactions to what I see, I know it is a story, a fabrication, and I know I am separated from the action. I do not believe in it." But gradually curiosity and then belief draw the spectator away from disbelief, and during the process of the first act—moment by moment—he begins to believe what the actor is doing. He is still aware of himself—aware of his comfort, aware of the recent past, aware of his critical evaluation of the performance—but once in a while, here and there, he is drawn into the belief that the actors really mean what they are saying.

In the second act, belief draws him in further. His curiosity begins to take over. His doubt slowly gives way, and he is drawn further into belief. Now and then he finds himself involved for two or three minutes at a time. He finds himself actually captivated by the actors and by what they are saying and doing. For periods of time, he even believes them to be who they say they are. Then toward the end of the second act, he relinquishes more control; without realizing it, he finds himself believing a prolonged passage just before the fall of the second-act curtain. During the intermission he is eager to learn how the third act will be resolved. He returns to his seat, and hardly ten or twelve lines of the third act have been spoken before his belief in the action is almost continuous. He believes the actors to be who they say they are, and he believes they mean what they are saying. He believes they are in the trouble they say they are in, and believes that they feel true emotional distress. Relentlessly his belief draws him further under the spell, and without any noticeable transition, he believes himself to be the character he is watching. He believes that he is in the same trouble that the actor is in. He believes that he and the actor are one.

Now he is drawn into a few moments of what we might call complete absorption—a period of partially unconscious experience. That's a very important characteristic of what we have referred to as the last seven minutes. In fact, for one spectator it may be only thirty seconds or a minute, and for another, the period of deep absorption may be as long as twenty to thirty minutes. For purposes of discussion, we'll assume the experience lasts an average of about seven minutes.

Now to review quickly, the major characteristic of this seven-minute period is that belief has drawn the viewer into complete absorption, an unconscious experience during which he loses track of himself. He doesn't know who he is anymore. He has relinquished critical judgment. He has abandoned himself. He is lost in the play and his belief systems have conquered him completely. He believes he is in danger just as the actor is in danger. He believes he needs what the actor needs. He hopes for what the actor hopes for. There is complete identification between the actor and him. He believes himself to *be* the actor. He is now in a state of awe at something outside himself; and what is more, he is not aware that this transaction has taken place.

As the final speeches of the play are being spoken, he becomes dimly aware that the play is drawing to a close. In the last few moments of the play, when the resolution is in sight, his critical faculties gradually return. Slowly he becomes aware again of his separateness. A sense of relief and satisfaction take over as the curtain falls and he finds himself returning to his individual reality.

Only then does he become aware of having had the experience of complete unity. What happened was that through the medium of belief his consciousness transcended to a state in which he was in complete unity with something outside himself. During that phase he was completely unaware of his physical comfort, his future, his past, his problems, his longings—everything about his life was completely surrendered to an identification with the actor's belief. This experience of unity is rare and special. Most people regard it as enjoyable, charming, healthful, spiritually renewing, even inspiring; this moment of unity is usually experienced as refreshing, and once experienced, most spectators look forward to frequent repetition.

This transcendence into unity is the mark of a work of art in the theatre. The more prolonged the moment of unified belief, the more powerful the work of art; what happened was that an audience of, let us say, a thousand spectators was more or less simultaneously drawn into a state of unity consciousness. When one is in this state, one is not aware of the experiencing self. The characteristic of unity consciousness is that one is aware of it only *after* it has happened. One looks back on it in this way: "I don't remember anything specifically about that seven minutes. I don't remember being worried or happy or confused or eager during that seven minutes; I don't remember anything except the general feeling of having been absorbed. I didn't know who I was, I lost track of time, I didn't have a care in the world, I was completely *in* it, I was on the edge of my seat, I was captivated, I was compelled, I was enthralled, I was spellbound." One might describe it in all these ways, but the observation one fails to make is, "For those few moments, my consciousness transcended to a state of perfect unity." Of course, if a fire alarm sounded during that seven minutes, the spell would immediately be broken; the belief systems would collapse, and unity would give way once again to multiplicity.

What we are describing are two different levels of consciousness—the experience of which is the mystery, or magic, of theatre. These moments of unity, in which the audience and the actors are one, are the very purpose and the reward of drama. Theatre people will endure considerable hardship and suffering in hopes of attaining even a few moments of this unity. But because these sacred experiences are irrelevant to the practical actions of our profession, this unity—which is a result, not a goal—is never referred to.

Theatre artists would be appalled to hear such ideas spoken aloud. We are magicians, not metaphysicians. The actor, who always covers his tracks, would respond with an offhand remark such as, "So you like the show, eh?" An actor would never openly admit that a play is an innocent masquerade that uses the power of belief to draw the spectator into a few moments of unity consciousness.

# Intuition, Creativity, Positation

## INTUITION

Intuition is the most important component of the creative process. Intuition is perfect. My intuition is perfect. Your intuition is perfect. All intuition is perfect. Spontaneous right thought and automatic right and appropriate action become manifest through the apparatus of intuition. The intuition is the uncluttered avenue by which perfection makes itself available to human perception. Intuition is the path by which perfect Universe travels into individual human experience. It is the most efficient mechanism by which "absolute" becomes expressed in the "relative."

It is generally agreed that the work of the human brain falls into two major classifications. Under the term "critical brain" we will include aspects of thought such as rationality, judgment, decision-making, analytical process, exactitude, self-discipline, value standards, selection, memory, willpower, logic, and discretion. Some psychologists have postulated that these characteristics are housed in the "left brain."

Under the term "intuitive brain" we will include characteristics such as emotion, hunches, flights of fancy, imagination, sensory experience, parapsychological experience, instinct, genius, inspired ideas, dreams, daydreams, aspirations, humor, caprice, playfulness, artistic sensitivity, and illogical responses. These are the aspects that some contemporary psychologists group together as representing the action of the "right brain." The intuitive brain is like an oversized retarded child playing with a bauble and mumbling incoherent phrases. It acts like a baby, it wants its own way in everything, it requires perpetual attention, it is unreliable and completely unreasonable. But within that moronic child lives the brilliant composer of dreams. Dreams are arrangements of poetically perfect, preciously interlocking, self-referential symbols. There is a quality of perfect creation in a dream. That perfect poetic creativity is the work of the little genius, or the "little professor," sitting in the intuitive brain. In other words, the intuitive brain is the home of an amorphic moron who is selfish, moody, and irresponsible, but who, on certain occasions, is inspired with flashes of brilliant and unassailably right thought, flawlessly appropriate action, and sublime clarity of vision. Intuition is capable of inspiring one with instant truth, with absolute and perfect clarity. It is ironic that intuition, the source of inspiration and genius, should spend most of its time behaving "like a slob."

Now, critical brain usually attempts to discipline the intuitive brain. Critical brain decides to give up cigarettes and chocolates. Critical brain resolves to do the right thing. Being logical and decisive, it is always trying to persuade intuitive brain to "behave." Intuitive brain has bad manners. Intuitive brain laughs in church. It is a common misbelief in Western thought that left brain can achieve everything, especially when it is able to tyrannize right brain. But in the creative process, the freedom of right brain is tremendously precious to us because right brain contains the little genius. In the creative process, we seek to encourage the intuitive brain. We have to make friends with intuition. We have to let intuition know that it will be trusted at every moment, and that whenever intuition feeds us something, we are going to *respect* it and *use* it no matter what our critical faculties think.

Now, a director gives this message to the actor: "I will use your creative thoughts no matter what they are. Any thoughts that you give me I will use." Intuition, the moronic child, hears the message. At first, the intuition will not believe the message. The wayward right brain will send down some insolent and inappropriate idea just to test the director—to prove the director a liar. The director patiently uses the first idea no matter how clumsy and coarse it may seem. Now, when the actor's intuition realizes that his coarse suggestion has actually been put to use, the intuition mutters, "I can't believe he used that moronic idea. I'll send him down a worse one and see what he makes of that!" The director unquestioningly uses the second idea that the actor's intuitive process delivers, thus sending the message back to the intuition, "You have suggested two ideas and both ideas have been used." The intuition falls into careful reflection, mumbling, "What is this? A game? A trick? Or could there be a pattern here?" When the director uses the third suggestion of the actor's intuition without modifying, questioning, or quibbling, the intuition locks into a very important realization. This realization will significantly affect the work of the director in relation to the actor's creative intuition.

## THE LEARNING PROCESS

We learn in threes. The first step of learning is discovering; the second step of learning is testing; and the third step of learning is pattern-setting. The actor's intuitive brain has tested the director twice: "The director has used my creative idea both times, but will he use the third?" Once again, the actor's intuition sends down a creative idea. He is very alert now, waiting for the director's response. The director, with unqualified enthusiasm, uses the third idea and presto: The pattern is set. Thus, the actor's intuition has gone through the three steps of learning. He sets the pattern and establishes this understanding: "Everything I send down will be used by the director; he'll even use the bad and mediocre ideas." Now, this is the message the director wants to get through to the actor's "little genius." The message he wants to get through to that moronic and irresponsible intuitive creativity is that "everything you send down will be respected and *used.*"

Intuition now becomes lively. It becomes excited and challenged. "Since everything I'm sending down is being used, why not send down the A-material?" Now the actor's intuition starts sending down his good ideas because he knows that everything is going to be used, that nothing is going to be wasted or rejected. By using this technique, the director pulls the intuition of the actor out of its distrust, out of its laziness, its defensiveness, and its defiance. He has drawn the actor's intuition out of the lusterless selfishness in which it customarily wallows. The director has shone light on the actor's intuition. "Everything that intuition delivers is not only useful, it is beautiful."

From now on the actor's intuition becomes the ally of the director and will deliver one creative idea after another. The ideas will become more appropriate, more effective, even more inspired, and there will be very few "bad" ideas anymore.

The challenge in this technique lies in the director's ability to use the actor's first three ideas, no matter what they are, no matter how stupid or ridiculous they may seem to be—to use them without question, without derogation, and without reservation, to use the ideas *as they are delivered.* This requires that the director be disciplined and very creative.

Even when the idea seems to be completely unworkable, a mature director can live with it for a few days, because a bad idea will eventually fall out of orbit by its own weight. Why get into an argument with an actor over an early idea, awakening all his critical, intellectual forces? You want to avoid an intellectual contest with the critical brain. You want to persuade the intellect to "come along for the ride." You want to encourage the intuitive brain to give anything it wants to give. After it has delivered three very clumsy ideas as tests and the director has used all three clumsy ideas and used them with respect, the actor will never deliver another clumsy idea. From now on the actor will deliver only good ideas—creative intuitive flow. After seventeen or eighteen ideas have been fed into the process, then the path is prepared for the inspired idea.

The actor now feels enriched, exhilarated by the realization that everything he contributes is being used. That's when intuition says, "Why am I holding back? Why don't I send down the glory?" That's when the universally right idea is delivered unfettered, untroubled, undiluted, unmixed, uncluttered, unsullied, pure and perfect. Universe just pours straight through the intuition in its most clear and most appropriate form. The artist is the conduit by which Universe expresses itself, and it is the artist's job to open the channel for that expression. The channel by which Universe expresses itself directly is through perfect, pure, clear, innocent intuition. The material may be explained by the critical brain, but the critical brain merely organizes things after the fact; the intuitive brain is the creative source.

The most important thing a director can do for an actor is to awaken the actor's intuition and assure the intuition that it is going to be witnessed and used. How can the actor's intellect, which is so vigilant and so exacting, learn to accept and trust the intuition so noted for unreliability? The critical and intuitive functions must learn to become friends. They must come into harmony and then they become coincident. During the truly creative process, the artist is aware of a sense of great personal stillness. He is dealing in the moment. When the critical and intuitive brain are working together, the sense of absorption is intense. The sense of fun is intense, as well. During the truly creative process, the creator is essentially unaware of anything, almost unconscious of his surroundings, oblivious to past or future, and totally unaware of the passage of time.

Now, when one is working out one's income tax, one relies a great deal on the pure intellect. When one is directing a play, the critical judgment and the intuition work together. When acting, the actor allows himself to rely very heavily on emotion and impulse. The critical faculty agrees to lie back and be less exacting. Essentially, an actor says, "I will trust the director to function in the capacity of my critical brain while I give my intuitive brain full opportunity to express. I will rely on the director to keep me from looking foolish. I will put my intellectual responsibilities into the director's care in order to permit my intuition to act and be creative."

Let's look at it another way. Every human act is a creative act. There is no such thing as a noncreative act. Everything that happens is directly responsible to creativity. Every human event has been imaged into existence. The most enjoyable activities are the ones in which intuitive brain participates in a congenial way. When "left" and "right" brain are working together in harmony, all activities are enjoyable and one feels fulfilled. The greatest difficulty occurs when the critical brain exercises an unremitting tyranny over the intuitive brain. So, frequently, the intellect takes a disciplinary stance, a position of exactitude, tyrannizing the carefree action of emotions and impulses. If we encourage enough caprice, enough carelessness in our lives, the critical and intuitive aspects of brain will probably get along in a cooperative and agreeable fashion.

In summary then, we say that intuition is perfect. We say intuition is perfect because it is Universe making itself manifest through individual expression. It is perfect because it is the shortest, clearest path by which absolute right knowledge expresses itself in the experience of the human being. Intuitive knowledge is always absolutely right. It is impulsive and inviolable. Anyone unaware of this truth is probably clutching too desperately to his intellect. Those who cannot relinquish the stranglehold that their critical judgment exercises over their wayward impulses are probably locked in an ego-bind. Such individuals are ill equipped for leadership in creative endeavors such as playmaking.

## POSITATION

By the principle of positation *we say yes to every creative idea.* We accept this principle as a discipline because we have found that doing so yields practical results. What we are talking about has nothing to do with morality; it has nothing to do with ethics. We do not say yes to everything for virtue's sake. We say yes because we understand that to do so is the practical way of sending a message to the intuition that every creative idea will be valued, respected, and used; and when the intuition gets that message often enough, it will send us its most perfect and its most pure creative ideas. That is why, whether we like it or not, saying yes to everything is the most creative technique an artist can employ.

When a painter is painting by himself, all alone, he has a tendency to "agree with himself" while he is working. But an actor, being in a social situation, has to agree not only with himself but with the director and the other actors. If we can persuade all the individuals in this collaborative art to work within the same system, that is, the system of respect for the intuition—the system of positation—the collective unconscious flourishes. Everyone's ideas will be vibrant and appropriate. Success will be inevitable. Everything that is spoken in a rehearsal will be regarded as useful. We acknowledge that even a suggestion made by the doorman arises from an intuitive source and could represent the long-looked-for missing piece in the puzzle. Even if a member of the chorus mutters something in passing, it is useful and right. In this manner the director begins to allow Nature to aid him in directing the play.

## NATURE AS ALLY

Nature feeds right and appropriate ideas into life in the same way that intuition feeds right and appropriate ideas into dreams. When a director acquires experience in this technique, the event of the rehearsal becomes a series of suggestions from perfect intuition, and he finds himself valuing and using every suggestion. This puts the director in harmony with Nature, because he is agreeing to use everything that Nature provides. When Nature perceives that you are using everything it provides, Nature streamlines what it feeds you. It begins to feed you only what is useful, supportive, and appropriate. It doesn't fling clutter in your path any longer. Nature begins to behave the same way that intuition behaves. It realizes, "I'm being trusted, I'm being used, everything that occurs is becoming part of the creative process." Therefore, Nature becomes more supportive and more cooperative, and starts to send you only appropriate opportunities. Nature has the power to select and feed in these stimuli in such a way that they arrive in the form of perfect poetic expression; they come with right intensity, timing, and coloration, and they are always appropriate. Essentially, Nature is your partner and everything that occurs is useful—with Nature as our constant ally, all our questions are answered; our needs are satisfied and our desires are fulfilled.

When you have the intuition of the actor as your ally, as well as the coincidence of Nature and Universe, which longs to be witnessed, the likelihood is that what you are developing will become a work of art. A work of art is inevitable because you have these three powerful sources providing you with material—the individual intuition, Nature, and Universe. You've opened up the channels and your success is inevitable. Success cannot be avoided. The more you interpose your self—ego or left-brain activity—the greater disharmony you are likely to cause. It's important for a director to know when to keep his mouth shut. It's more important for a director to remain silent than to speak. Don't say something just because there's an empty space. If you are not certain what to say, always postpone, because the postponement itself represents a message to intuition that you are waiting for the right knowledge to come down. Then intuition sends you the right knowledge; you recognize it instantly and there is no hesitation before you speak. "Oh, in that case, what we need here is . . ." You started speaking even before you realized it. Intuition made the rightness of the idea so appealing that you blurted it out. Allow your intuition to command you. Never force yourself. Never allow yourself to feel obliged to speak.

In dealing with actors it is essential for the director to understand the creative process; to trust and encourage the intuition; to use all the events of nature, everything that happens in the rehearsal itself, in order to clear the path so that Universe may express itself.

There are techniques for dealing with intuition and positation. The consistent use of these techniques makes it unnecessary for a director to use very many other techniques. A great deal of time and verbiage can be saved, and a flood of left-brain confusion can be avoided if you learn how to use your intuition with respect and how to enlist the harmonic cooperation of the intuition of the actors.

Remember that if anyone asks you a question, that question is your guidance. When an actor asks a question, it is not the answer he seeks. The answer to the question is in the question. The question is merely a blameless way of drawing attention to something unresolved. Give attention to the unresolved, but don't answer the question. Ask more questions, and let the actor answer the question. Never answer a question. Always ask for an answer, because when an actor asks a question, he already, intuitively, knows the best answer. "How should I do it, on the right or the left?" "Which way is best?" "If I do it on the right, I can get there in time. If I do it on the left, it won't work." "Well, then do it on the right." The answer to the question is in the question. The actor's answer will be organic, and you won't have imposed anything. It doesn't work imposing your will on a production and then having to live with the results. Eventually, you'll look at it and say, "Oh, what a mess. It is all filled with me and I hate it."

As a director, emphasize the creative. Keep saying yes to the ideas and don't talk too much. Use just a few phrases. The reason you don't speak much is that what is to be created cannot be easily packaged in language. If you talk about it, it will get heavy, mired in left-brain terminology. If you haven't said anything today, someone's intuition may come up with a brilliant suggestion tomorrow. But if you wedge some left-brain thought into the work today, tomorrow you are going to have to pull it out before the intuition can flow easily. In order to awaken the creative process at the beginning of the rehearsal the director might say, "I know you are all superior actors, well suited to your roles. And we have a beautiful play to work on. Let's begin at the beginning and read for sense and see what we can discover." You don't have to say any more than that. After that, all you have to do is listen and say yes. Remember, you can't play all the parts yourself. The actor can play the part better than you can. Let him do the work. Make it easier for him. Clear the obstacles from his path. Most actors feel as though a script is an obstacle course. Help him find the path.

The path we are looking for, the actor and the director together, is the inner life of the character. The director's responsibility is to evoke and discover that inner life. A director who imposes things on his actors is usually giving them obstacles and is frustrating or binding their creative processes. That's why we say, Impose as little as possible. Speak as little as possible. Encourage as much as possible. Say yes to everything. Allow Nature to work for you.

# The Cornerstones
# for Success

## BELIEF IN THE GENERAL BEAUTY

If as a director you are going to spend four or five weeks in rehearsal, the play should be something you consider worthy of your time, something you find fascinating. During this period, you will be doing a lot of exploring and investigating; you will be carrying creative thoughts about the play with you all day, every day, for a long time. The play therefore must *excite* you.

Now we come to the use of a phrase that has become traditional to several generations of directors but which is so vague as to seem almost meaningless. The word "beauty" has become unspecific and is rendered even more vague when we describe it as "general." And yet this blousy term *general beauty* is one of the cornerstones of successful stage direction.

Let us see if we can circumscribe the general beauty in order to give it meaning. If we consider general beauty to be the sack, some of the potatoes that will fill it and make it stand up are: What does a play represent? What is its theme? Why is it important? Why does it deserve to be witnessed? What is the moral? What universal truth does it illustrate? What excites you the director about the work? What aspect of the drama fires your imagination? What makes you feel zealous and impassioned?

What moves you? What about the material gives you a deep feeling of satisfaction? What in the play makes it worthy of an audience's attention? Why is it compelling?

In order to standardize the terms of our techniques, I subscribe to the traditional if somewhat fuzzy phrase "general beauty" to designate the aspect of a play that awakens a director's subjective enthusiasm. The general beauty embodies the theme and the moral that the play represents.

If you are not excited about a play, throw it out even if you are offered an immense salary to direct it. If your best friend says, "Will you direct a play in which I long to appear?" and you are not sold lock, stock, and barrel on the merit of the play, throw it out. As a director you cannot succeed in something in which you do not believe. It is impossible.

Now, having said that, it is sometimes possible to convince yourself to believe in something with qualifications. Occasionally, you will not think too much of a play on first reading, but on rereading and rethinking, you sense that there are certain aspects of the material that could be developed. The material might offer you an opportunity to develop some aspect of your work that you have never had a chance to explore. It is impossible, however, to go into rehearsal with the belief that what you are about to direct is not beautiful.

The general beauty of a work is the way in which we talk about its worthiness to be seen. The general beauty contains the theme. The general beauty is the reason we feel passionately that an audience should see it. The general beauty is what excites the director and what makes him feel that other people should be excited. A director has to be a missionary. He must feel strongly about the theme of a play—to the extent that he feels it is important for other people to share or to witness that theme. He has to feel that civilization will be enhanced and society will be enriched if the message of that play is revealed. He has to feel that the play is a tool to awaken people to values that he personally feels are important. If the director does not feel that the values revealed in a play are important, he cannot commit himself to it with any degree of success. So we say that the general beauty is what the director looks for when he first reads the script. Sometimes the general beauty appears as a mere thread, and the director will say, "I can turn that thread into a rope, into a cable, and then into a battering ram of meaning." On the other hand, sometimes he says, "I can see a thread of general beauty, but by the time the producer, the designers, and the stars have staked out their ego rights to this play, the thread is going to disappear into a cobweb, then into a wisp, and soon it is likely to be lost completely." In that case, he would do well to leave it alone.

The director must believe. We are makers of belief. The director is the one who believes first. I do not mean he believes the story to be true—which is also an important belief to have—but he must believe in what the story represents. He has to believe that he could stand on the corner and sell it, that he could market it, that he could convince people of the beauty, that he could stop passersby and say, "Did you ever wonder about the possibility of this? Isn't this beautiful? Doesn't this strike you as something important and marvelous and amazing and peculiar and wonderful?" The likelihood of success is almost nil if the director doesn't believe in the theme. He must be able to commit his sense of vision to it. In his mind he should have clearly filled in the blanks in statements like, "This play is worthy of the attention of an audience because . . ." or "Everybody in the world should be aware that . . ." or "It will cheer everybody up to know that . . ." The general beauty involves everyone.

When a director chooses the general beauty, he is making a choice on behalf of the audience. The director agrees to represent the public. The identity of the director goes like this: "I am an audience, I am anybody, I am everyman, I am all, I am judge, I am servant, I am listener, I am moderator, I am synthesizer, I am seeker, I am helper, I am child, I am believer, and I am maker of belief." If you take a posture of being superior to your audience or inferior to them, you have done them and yourself a disservice. What you really want is to *be* them, and you spend most of your time as a director pretending that you are "anybody." "I am anyone who is able to give a fair amount of attention but not a lot; who has a fair amount of intelligence and a fair amount of curiosity, but not a lot." Take nothing for granted. Work for their attention and hold onto it. The minute the director is bored, the audience will be bored.

If you believe in the general beauty of the play, it will carry you zestfully through the rehearsal period. If you do not believe in the general beauty, you will be in misery. If you partially believe in it, you will get part of the way through the rehearsal and things will begin to break down. You will start getting angry with the actors; you will start blaming people for things they haven't done; you will notice yourself feeling resentful, uncertain, isolated.

It doesn't matter whether an actor walks to the left or to the right of the sofa, and it doesn't make any difference whether his shoes are beige or black. But it does make a difference whether or not you have chosen a play that you believe in. The early and big decisions are the ones that count. You will be unable to rescue the situation later on if you have made the wrong decisions at the beginning; and belief in the general beauty of the play is the earliest and most important decision of all.

## TRADITIONAL FORM

There are traditions in playwriting that a director has to understand in order to succeed. There is a tradition of playwriting in the following forms: tragedy, melodrama, high comedy, farce, satire, vaudeville, burlesque, propaganda, divertissement, circus, improvisation, night club, music hall, street show, puppet show, mime, opera, revue, musicale or musical comedy, operetta, movies, rite or ritual, happening, parade, lecture, reading, recital, contests or games, radio shows, television, rallies, speech-making and exhortation, children's tales, parties. As a director commences thought on a particular play, it is important to establish in which tradition the play lies. Sometimes it lies in a combination of one or two traditions. If you choose the wrong tradition, your production will quickly slide out of control. It will start kicking back and heaving loose ends and stray parts at you from every angle.

## PREDOMINANT ELEMENT

*Predominant element* is a somewhat academic term, but I use it as another handy phrase in preparing a script. Once you have decided to do a play, the second question that you ask yourself is, "What is the predominant element?" There are five possible answers. The predominant elements are theme, plot, character, spectacle, and language.

Many directors go into rehearsal without having decided on a predominant element. A director will find himself in trouble, for instance, when he has filled the stage with spectacle—wagons, elevators, scenery and flying pieces—only to realize that he is doing a play whose predominant element is language. In this case, the scenery overwhelms the language and the audience becomes the loser. Let us consider some examples of predominant element.

**Plot**    *The Tavern* by George M. Cohan is a play in which the predominant element is (almost exclusively) plot. The action hurls itself relentlessly at the audience mowing down all before it. Character is continuously subservient to plot, and the language is prosaic at best. The theme, Crime does not pay, is apparent from the beginning, and the spectacle requires only an upstage door and a winter wind so powerful it drives all the players to the wall. A triumph of plot.

**Character**    All the plays of Chekhov have the predominant element of character. One could barely choose plot as the secondary element. It is unlikely that one would choose language, because the language in Chekhov is intentionally commonplace. An academician might insist that there is theme in Chekhov, but it is so subservient to character, it is so low in the play and rises so gracefully and gently to the surface, that we say, essentially, that Chekhov is without theme. In Chekhov's plays we go for character, with secondary emphasis on plot, because one must keep the action moving or the audience will fall asleep.

**Theme**  *Waiting for Lefty* by Clifford Odets is a thesis play directly promoting the theme that the common man will continue to be oppressed until he succeeds in organizing into unions. It is nearly a propaganda play. Character and dialogue serve the theme exclusively. The spectacle is limited to a bare stage. The language is didactic to the point of preachiness. This is a play, great in its time, whose theme has become irrelevant. It offers little else to recommend contemporary performance.

**Spectacle**  *Barnum* by Mark Bramble and Michael Stewart won a number of prizes in New York, despite the fact that it has no plot, no characters of consequence, and no significant language; its theme, at best, could be stated, A circus causes sweat. Nevertheless, the sheer intensity and speed of the spectacle, the unrelenting energy, the nonstop sensation of movement, sound, and color; the surprises, the acrobatic feats, dances, magic, and razzmatazz overwhelmed and gratified audiences. Spectacle provided this production with a long Broadway run.

**Language**  *Under Milk Wood* by Dylan Thomas is subtitled "A Play for Voices." It is a demonstration of the most miraculous parade of words in spoken English. It is poetry at its most dazzling. The theme is vague at best: something like, Isn't life a terrible thing, thank God! or Ordinary people are sublime. As for plot, it is a patchwork of incidents involving sixty-four characters in a tiny Welsh town in the course of a summer day. The characters are sketched, not developed. The predominant element in this play is clearly the most radiant language ever assembled, seconded possibly by the perfect miniatures of character. Spectacle would ruin this work, as would any attempt to lean on theme or plot.

**Mixtures**  The examples cited above are plays demonstrating one predominant element to the exclusion of the other four.

Most plays have a bit of all five and a preponderance of one. The great exceptions, of course, are the plays of our father, the master playwright, greatest mind in Western civilization—Shakespeare. One reason his works tower so far above all others is that he fuses the elements of theme, plot, character, spectacle, and language so magnificently. In Shakespeare, we marvel at the great skill with which these elements have been united. For example, in *Hamlet* the language, verse, and thought are unparalleled in Western expression. Character—the sensitive prince surrounded by exquisitely detailed and complex family members, friends, and adversaries. Plot—ghosts demanding vengeance, schemes of murder, love betrayed, poisoned swords, mistaken slayings, suicides, conspiracies; enough plot for a handful of plays. Theme—The story of a young man who cannot make up his mind, or A sensitive mind is overwhelmed by external circumstances, or Every man must resolve the internal conflict between intellect and passion, between reason and blood, or The gods require vengeance when a just ruler is slain. There are as many different themes in *Hamlet* as there are productions. And as for spectacle, the play is a showman's field day: the ghost appearing and disappearing on the battlement; the royal displays at court; the play within a play; an opportunity to slay a monarch while he is praying; murder in a mother's bedroom; the violent repudiation of an innocent girlfriend—a teenage maiden, mad with grief, strewing flowers about; a young romantic, holding a skull, considering mortality; a prince dueling publicly with envenomed swords; a queen erringly drinking a chalice of poison; and the arrival of a royal young warrior when the stage is littered with dead bodies. The opportunities for spectacle are limited only by the imagination of the director. So we see in Shakespeare a complexity that is difficult to narrow to one predominant element.

From observation and experience, I maintain that if a director allows himself the indulgence of including all five elements at the same time, he will overwhelm both himself and the production. To allow four predominant elements is also unwieldy and will baffle the audience and cause disunity among the players. Even wise directors who take on three elements, allowing equal emphasis to each, usually turn out a vague and diffuse presentation, no matter how fine the play. I believe that narrowing one's focus and being specific and creative within limitation leads to the most vivid success. That is why I choose one predominant element and stick to it with the exactitude of a monk, allowing a secondary element to mention itself gracefully, at appropriate moments.

## WORLD OF THE PLAY

No two plays, even by the same author, are the same. Nor should any two plays be directed in the same way. The director's goal is to realize the vision of the author and persuade the actors of the enjoyability of entering into the world of that vision. Some theatre people refer to the word "style," but I avoid using it because it is vague and misleading. Critics, who are amateurs anyway, will occasionally comment, "So-and-so is a style actor," or "So-and-so is skilled at directing style plays," or "So-and-so has great style in his direction."

I have been asked to direct new scripts with the inducement, "This play is special and it needs your particular style to bring it off." Invariably this meant that the script was in real trouble and in need of a rescue.

Style is a word like emotion. It is so confusing that we omit it from our daily theatrical parlance. But, in place of the word style, we use the phrase "the world of the play."

Every play has its own world. Some plays have fuzzy worlds, incomplete worlds, inconsistent worlds, hard-to-handle or hard-to-grasp worlds. Let's not talk about lopsided worlds of the play for a minute. Let's talk about well-formed worlds of the play.

The world of the play limits a play as a frame limits a picture. It limits the action. It is important for the director not to put anything into the play that doesn't belong within that frame. For example, if you were painting a miniature of Queen Elizabeth in a sixteenth-century setting, you wouldn't put an airplane in the background. If you were enacting a version of Picasso's *Guernica*, you wouldn't introduce a man carrying pies across the foreground because you would be violating the world of the play. Each play has its world, and what belongs in that world is consonant to it. Everyone, even children, can immediately spot something that doesn't belong in the world of a play.

There is a children's game that shows certain objects in an arrangement. The child is asked, "What object does not belong in this arrangement?" The picture might be a kitchen and everything in the kitchen seems appropriate except for a goat that is standing in the sink. The child says, "Oh, the goat doesn't belong in the sink." This old game helps teach children how to recognize samenesses and differences.

Directors have to be experts at samenesses and differences. In order to achieve a consonant world of the play, we put samenesses together and leave differences out.

Now, of course, immediately I have to say that there are exceptions; occasionally, we create an entire production full of sameness; then suddenly, at a special moment, we introduce one triumphant difference, which can be very dramatic. Secretly, however, we have prepared the audience so that they unconsciously expect the difference and accept it with satisfaction.

But let us not talk about the exceptions before we have discussed the rule itself. Creating the world of the play means gathering together those objects and manners that are like each other, or that are consonant. Putting the samenesses together and bringing harmony to the component parts is the business of the director. He must be vigilant in keeping out the differences, the things that don't belong. Sometimes a director will limit himself deliberately. For instance, "Everything in this play will be beige, oatmeal, and straw colored." By limiting everything to this sameness, he creates a very specific and connotative world. If he says, "I want the world of the play to represent authentic life in the village of Ivanova in Russia, 160 miles from Moscow, in the winter of 1897," then he has created a naturalistic world of the play that prohibits the inclusion of all other possibilities.

## WORLD OF THE PLAY COMPOSED OF SYSTEMS

One of the greatest errors directors make is what I call "breaking systems." This means that having established a pattern of systems, the director foolishly introduces a single detail that violates his own systems. Here is an example. I once saw a production of *The Three Sisters*. A great deal of effort was made to give it systems of authenticity. Nineteenth-century costumes, oil lamps, genuine military uniforms, authentic crystal decanters, and period cameras were used. At the end of the first act, one of the actors presented a contemporary toy, a top, to Irina. By the chromium design and the computerized buzz, the audience could easily see that the top was a creation of the 1970s. By using one contemporary toy, the director had violated his own systems of authenticity, and all his work to achieve integrated naturalism in the first act was destroyed. That one moment of disbelief suddenly brought the entire act crashing to the floor. It is astounding how frequently, and with what apparent casualness, directors destroy their own systems.

If, in creating the world of the play, you set up a system, you must be *absolute* in obedience to that system. You cannot change the system whenever it occurs to you, or whenever a variation for effect would be interesting. The director must forbid himself such shabby indulgence. If you want an authentic production, then the world of the play that you are creating must be inviolately authentic. You might say, "The world of the play is a dream, a vague memory, and therefore certain things happen with fuzzy borders." In this instance the director establishes the dream qualities of that world right from the beginning and finds ways of preserving the dreaminess of that world all the way through to the end. When you are establishing the world of the play, seek within the heart of the play for the most revealing world. What will reveal the playwright most clearly? What will heighten the playwright's ideas most clearly? What will make them most accessible to the audience?

The playwright frequently spells out the kind of world that he wants. The director can either accept that world or succeed by imposing an entirely strange and different world on the play. Some examples of creating the world of the play:

> Katharine Hepburn had great success setting *Much Ado About Nothing* in Mexico in the late 1800s.
>
> A.C.T. placed *The Taming of the Shrew* in the world of commedia dell'arte very effectively.
>
> In *Arturo Ui* by Brecht the world of the play is dictated by what is frequently called newspaper style. The playwright has called for historic headlines; cartoonlike events; prototypic characters, and a bold, single-dimensional reality. The world of the play written into the text is didactic—it is hard, flat, and posterlike. If a director attempts to introduce revealing human detail or warm and likeable humor into this play, he is violating the world of the play.
>
> In *Charley's Aunt* the world of the play is composed of unlikelihoods and broken Victorian conventions. The more believably one can saturate the play with these unlikelihoods and the more frequently one can break the established conventions, the more delightful the world of the play becomes.
>
> Some time ago I saw a production of *As You Like It* with an all-male cast. The world of the play was composed of plastic, chrome, and polka dots. The director may create any world he desires. The important thing is that whatever world he creates must remain integrated, consonant, and obedient to the rules of its own systems.

## METAPHOR

I would like to discuss for a moment a technique that I did not fully understand or utilize until somewhat late in my career. Since that time, it has been so useful to me that I would never be without it while directing a play. The use of this technique could be summarized as the concept of having a metaphor for the production.

We all know that a simile is a direct comparison. The use of "as" or "like" is expected in this figure of speech. For example, "He runs as fast as the wind," or "His rage is like a thunderstorm."

In metaphor, however, the words "like" and "as" are omitted, so that the comparison is more striking. "His smile is pure sunshine." "He is a tornado around the office."

Now let us extend the concept of metaphor so that it includes an entire production. We are looking for some object, picture, statement, photograph, sketch, or fabric that shall not only be like the production, but, in the director's mind, shall be the production itself. To make this very clear, let me use some illustrations:

- *The Visit* by Duerrenmatt is "a nightmare of sadistic power."
- *Thieves' Carnival* by Anouilh is "a vanilla-and-strawberry ice-cream sundae."
- *The Bald Soprano* by Ionesco is "a household of robots."
- *The Girl of the Golden West* by Belasco is "a daguerreotype print."
- *Ah, Wilderness!* by O'Neill is a "memory of Norman Rockwell."
- *The Circle* by Maugham is a "delicate celadon oriental vase."
- *The Dance of Death* by Strindberg is "a cockfight."

The metaphor limits the way a director thinks about the play. Usually, the limitation is a physical one.

When preparing a new production, I usually ask a director to find a photograph or a painting that most clearly symbolizes to him the entire concept of the play. Then I ask him to limit the production of the play to the colors, the textures, and the tone of that picture. This introduces a limitation on color that some people have called "color coordination" or "limited palette." It also introduces a limitation on texture, as in a production whose metaphor is described by the lavendar lace and silk bows of a Victorian greeting card; or as in a production that is limited to straw and packing boards, or to leather and bronze. When one chooses a metaphor for a production, one limits the terms of expression. One limits the color, silhouette, texture, movement, timing, and the degree and kind of reality. This limitation is creative. Its great advantage is that it keeps out a lot of extraneous and unmatched ingredients. The discipline of following one metaphor requires the director to unify his thoughts.

Exercising great discipline in conforming to one metaphor tends to give the production visual unity, consistency, and power. Without a metaphor, one is working at random with unlimited resources of color, line, texture. In such productions, the fact that the ingredients are unlimited causes the work to look like a shamble of accidents. Since we seek unity in a work of art, there is a great advantage in using a device that forces unity into the production. There should be only one metaphor—a painting, for instance. More than one metaphor would be immediately confusing and disunifying.

If I use Rembrandt's *The Night Watch* as the metaphor for a production, the colors of the clothing and the quality of light in the picture will limit the colors and the lights of the production. The movement and groupings will suggest movement and groupings for the stage. The textures will dictate the costumes and background. By choosing this metaphor, I eliminate from the scenery and props many colors, lines, and textures. I do not say the production will be somewhat like *The Night Watch* or in the manner of *The Night Watch*, I say the production will be *The Night Watch* as it is.

By using this technique, we come to understand one of the most important concepts in art: Limitation frees creativity. If a child is given unlimited time, unlimited money, unlimited space, and all the resources he could wish, his play will soon become dull. A child's play is always enhanced in creativity by the limitations imposed upon him. These limitations cause the game to come to life. Given unlimited space, time, and money, an artist will probably dawdle, and the focus of his work will disappear in the meanderings of indecision. Necessity is, in fact, the mother of invention, and limitation is the springboard of creativity.

In choosing a metaphor for a play, the director imposes limitations on himself and on the entire production from the beginning, and these limitations fire his creativity and the creativity of his designers and actors. These limitations ultimately provide the production with greater punch, clarity, meaning, unity, imagination, vigor, wit, power, invention. The metaphor is a limitation that pays off in extraordinary creativity.

I have learned from my own experience and from my observation of the work of other directors that the more clear and striking the metaphor, the more unified and powerful the production. The converse is also true. The more vague the metaphor, the more commonplace the production.

# Auditions and Casting

Casting is the major decision that a director makes. If you cast correctly, you have done about eighty percent of your work. This is why casting is so very delicate; it is as critical as a doctor's diagnosis. If you make the right diagnosis, the likelihood is that the patient will get well; but if you diagnose incorrectly, you are in all sorts of trouble. Consider that you have the wrong actor in the part: You will spend long hours explaining—trying to get something from the actor that he is unable to give. If you have an older woman cast as a seventeen-year-old girl, you can ask her to be fresh and energetic, but the more she tries, the more trouble she gets into. The right person in the role represents eighty percent of the work done well.

The question occurs in casting: Do you cast for "type" or do you cast for skill? This is a dangerous trap to most directors. Frequently, someone will come in to audition who looks and sounds precisely like the character and who may even give a reading that is so close to the performance that you say, "Oh, this is destiny. The part is written for this actor." Then in the interview and from his resume you learn that he has limited experience in certain kinds of parts, he has never carried a play before, and he has never played comedy. Another actor comes in who seems unlike the specific type you are seeking, and yet he has played many parts that are similar to the part you are casting. He has carried a play many times, he has control of his speech, he knows how to get laughs, he knows the rehearsal process, he is familiar with technical language, and he is a seasoned professional. The second actor may not seem to be the exact type that you had in mind for the part, but he is a professional actor.

Now, given these two actors, the perfect type and the skilled professional, which choice do you make? This is frequently a serious dilemma. My answer is, Always hire the skilled actor. Even though he doesn't seem the exact type, the skilled actor will always pull you through. If you hire the type, you will spend the entire rehearsal period begging and pleading and pulling teeth, and frustrating everyone else in the cast as well. Eventually, you come to the understanding that the type will never be able to hold his own. But you will always get a professional performance out of a skilled actor. I always favor the actor. You only have to make this mistake once in your career before you learn. The type is very elusive—the exceptions to this rule are "specialty casting" and "sight gags."

In casting, it is important to understand that when an actor walks into an audition, he is at his worst. He is nervous, he hopes he will land a job, he is in a strange place, and you are seen as the judge, the forbidding authority. His merit is on trial, he is probably unfamiliar with the material; he is all too aware of his shortcomings. His shoes are not shined; his collar is frayed; his hands are clammy; he has a slight cold; he hasn't studied the part and doesn't know what you're looking for. . . . In other words, the actor can be expected to appear in terrible condition at an audition. He's not in a position to be judged. As the auditioner, or casting director, you have certain humane responsibilities. As much as possible, you must relieve him of his apprehension. If you don't alleviate his anxiety, you won't get to know him at all. In that first few minutes it is important for you to get to know him very quickly. The first thing you have to do is put him at his ease and let him know that everything is forgiven in advance—that everything is okay.

My first interview with the great director Elia Kazan was extraordinary. As I walked in to the small room we shook hands and he immediately lay down on the floor. I hardly knew what to do, so I sat on the edge of a chair. As we talked about my resume he remained on the floor beside me. He understood that by lying on the floor he put me immediately and completely at ease in one deft gesture.

There are other techniques that I consider customary. You talk with an actor before you ask him to act; you allow him to spend two or three moments looking at faces and moving around the room and touching objects. It doesn't make too much difference what you talk about, but these few moments are precious to the actor.

When I ask the actor to begin his reading, I usually invite him to take off his shoes or to loosen his belt, or something inconsequential of that sort. It is a signal. Rarely does the actor accept the invitation to take off his shoes; but the somewhat silly suggestion carries with it this symbolic message: "In here, peculiar things are okay." If it is a reading, I always say, "Just read for sense, or just do it lightly once through. I want to hear your voice." This is to take the pressure off any need to perform. Then I usually say, "If you don't like what you're doing, stop and go back and start over." The reason I invite the actor to start over is to send the message that it is possible to get muddled and still be okay. He has to know that there is a way to get out of trouble. It reduces the pressure to know in advance that he can have a second chance. I think it is very important to have some key sentences that are short and that specifically target the actor's nervousness; we use these sentences from the minute the actor walks into the room.

Before the audition you shake hands. Courtesy is absolutely essential, and I mean more than just passing courtesy. The director must demonstrate respect and a certain kindness in the audition, because what the actor does is very difficult. It is humiliating for him. You never know at what stage of discouragement an actor comes to you. He may be close to giving up and your attitude may give him the encouragement needed to continue. I think of this as a rule: At the end of an audition, the actor should leave with a greater sense of self-esteem than when he came in. Even if you can't give him a job, you can upgrade his confidence. But you can't spend a great deal of time at it. You need short, deft sentences or rituals that send these signals quickly. It is very helpful at the end of an audition to touch the actor. There have been many studies revealing the powerful signals conveyed in touching—amazing that a short physical touch communicates confidence, friendliness, okayness, all sorts of messages.

How to ask the actor to begin his audition? I use sentences like, "What are you going to do for us?" or "Do something for us," because actors like to give. If they feel as though they are doing something for you, it opens up that channel. To begin the interview, I like the phrase, "Tell me something about yourself." The very next thing that the actor says can be one of the most revealing things about your future relationship. You listen very, very carefully. A doctor listens carefully when he questions a new patient for the first time. Doctors learn that the most important words they hear from a patient are the words that follow, "Well, what seems to be the trouble?" In our business, "Tell me something about yourself" is the same kind of invitation. At that moment the actor will fill in whatever happens to be pertinent to him; he will give you something from himself that he would like you to have. His phrasing is guidance for you on how to know him.

If you are a director, it is very helpful to have been an actor; every director should be required to audition whether or not he is a good actor. It is important for a director to experience the degree of panic that is involved and the feeling of desperation after auditioning.

Every time an actor auditions, it is imperative that the director thank him. He must be praised simply because he got through it. It took great courage. Whether it was good or not, you must convey the impression that he did well. That is your responsibility; there is no way you can get out of it.

It is very important not to mislead the actor at the end of the interview, because he lives on the hope that he takes out of that room. If, for instance, you say, "Your reading was better than anyone we've auditioned all day," he will go home thinking he has the part. What you haven't told him is that you plan to read for ten days and that he was actually too tall. It is better to keep your praise general.

It is also important not to try to be too popular, not to try to win votes with the actor. It is better not to give the actor anything to go on except that you will call him if, after thought, you consider that he's right.

At the close of the interview, you need another short set of phrases with an exact and unmistakable message. Many actors want to know, "If I get the part, how soon will you call me? Will you call me tomorrow? Will it be two weeks? Should I call you?" It is important to tell the actor how he will be notified if he has the part. He must be told what your plan is in as few words as possible. That's how the famous old expression "Don't call us, we'll call you" originated. It is quick and exact, but nowadays it is considered rude. I usually say something like, "Thank you. That was a very nice audition. We're meeting a number of people and when we see what our needs are, perhaps we'll be in touch with you."

## CASTING THE WRONG ACTOR

After casting an actor, do you have the right to change your mind? In Broadway theatre, the union contract provides a five-day clause. This means that the actor has five days to prove himself in the role. If he doesn't measure up, he can be fired without notice. I believe this procedure is inhumane and incorrect. If you engage an actor conditionally, he lives in fear of losing his job in the first five days; as a result, he gives you his least creative work because he's working in a state of fear. I look at it this way: As a professional director, you are expected to know what you are doing. When you audition an actor, you are supposed to be able to evaluate that actor's ability to play the part you have in mind. If you cast him in that part, that's a signification of your judgment. If you won't live with your own judgment, you are a shabby thinker. If I was wrong, I force myself to live with my decision. I am too stubborn to renege on my commitment. Here's another thought: It helps me to cast the right actor if I know that I will be irrevocably committed to that actor for the entire rehearsal period. I have to get to know him very well, until I know absolutely that this is the one person who can fully realize this role. If one makes a half-hearted commitment to the actor, one does the production a tremendous injustice. To replace an actor demoralizes everyone else in the company. Each feels that he may also be replaced. Putting in replacements is a tremendous waste of time. You need every moment of creative time for the rehearsal process. Other directors feel differently, but I feel very strongly that when you have hired an actor, he is yours until the opening. If he's the wrong actor for that part, it's your mistake. You live with it and you make it work. It represents unprofessionalism to fire an actor. It signifies essentially that the director admits he doesn't know what he is doing.

## HOW LONG SHOULD THE AUDITION BE?

I believe that if the actor has "psyched" himself up for an audition and has taken the time to prepare and to come all the way across town, he has the right to three minutes of acting time. In that three minutes, he can do anything he wants to do, and, in my opinion, you are obliged to listen. Frequently, you can tell that the actor is not meant for you in the first three sentences, but you must always let him complete the entire selection. He has probably worked hard on it, and it doesn't cost you much to sit there. You find yourself spending more time apologizing if you interrupt him than you would if you had let him finish peacefully. It is easier to sit there. It saves explanations. If you have been an actor, you wouldn't think of interrupting an audition. It is almost like a sacred rite.

## "TO WHOM DO I PLAY?"

If an actor plays to me during the audition, I pass my index finger in front of my eyes and direct his eye contact to some other place in the room. For film and television, casting directors like an actor to lean across the desk and play right to them. I prefer otherwise. I don't like an actor to oblige me to act with him, because I'm not there to act with him. I'm there to observe his acting. What if I suddenly yawn while he's playing to me? What if I turn to make a note on his resume while he's playing to me? I don't want to break his concentration, so I always say, "Play to the lamp shade," or "Play to the stage manager."

## COURTESY AUDITIONS

A courtesy audition is an agreement to see an actor whom you know in advance is not a likely candidate for the part, but whom you see at the suggestion of some connection—a friend or a relative—because it is easier to see him than it is to explain why you won't. A courtesy auditioner receives the exact same treatment that the other actors receive. Sometimes you discover some talent there, and occasionally you can say something encouraging that will get him to the next step.

# Relation to Actors

## FEAR

Fear is the primary enemy of creativity. When an actor approaches his role, it is always with some degree of fear. One of the jobs of the director is to encourage the actor to overcome his fear. Every director will find different techniques to supersede fear, but the most effective technique is for the director to assure the actor by what is said and done that they are allies; that the work will proceed on the basis of two people working toward a mutual goal.

The actor will learn to relinquish his fear when he sees that the director never causes another actor to be frightened. If the director terrorizes, victimizes, or humiliates someone else in the cast, an actor will automatically deduce, "That may happen to me one day," and his guard will be up perpetually. So, it is important for the director to have tremendous self-control. He must never send messages of derogation or contempt to any member of his cast, because as soon as the director sends one message like that, fear is awakened in the entire cast. It is essential that the director be the actor's ally, and each director must develop techniques that send messages quickly about that alliance—the kindness with which he speaks to actors, the way he touches them, the way he praises them, the way he always has time for their questions, the way he overlooks their mistakes. Fear has to be superseded if a director expects to get the best out of an actor.

## FAILURE

The greatest fear that an actor has is that he will fail in the part. All actors have that fear. At the beginning of the rehearsal process, I usually ask the assembled company, "Please think of the greatest successes you have had in your life and then think of the greatest failures. Which did you learn the most from, the failures or the successes?" Invariably, everyone has learned more from the failures. It is important to the creative process to recognize that we learn from our failures—much more than from our successes. Failure is the threshold of knowledge. Since new knowledge is that by which we progress, failure must be our constant companion. Every time we go through the doorway of knowledge, it is because we have stepped across a failure. We congratulate ourselves for failing. We fail boldly. We surround each other with love and enthusiasm after failure because we know that the failure took courage. On the other side of every failure is wisdom. Wisdom is growth, growth is progress, and progress is light. Failure is an integral part of life. Failure is a necessary and important part of the creative process. A director must encourage it and reward it, and he must tell actors in advance that he values their failures. Otherwise, the actor learns to live in fear of failure. If he fears failure, his creativity is seriously impaired and he will not grow. It is important to "Fail Big!"

## PRAISE

Each actor who enters the profession carries with him from childhood a starvation for approbation. As he grows older, he finds that acting is a socially acceptable form of doing something in hope of getting the kind of approval that he missed in his childhood. A director understands that to an actor praise is like food. The actor cannot live without it, cannot flourish without it. A director must discipline himself to praise ceaselessly.

It is not necessary for the actor to have done something extraordinary in order to be praised. General praise, in comments such as "You're doing nicely," or "This scene is coming along," or "It's a pleasure to work with you," doesn't have to apply to any specific achievement, but it lifts the actor's spirit and causes him to flourish. He feels his flower is blooming. He feels his life is healthy. He feels as though the sun is shining if a director, who is, after all, the authority figure, is in favor of him. Many children grow up in fear of, or in conflict with, their parents. Many actors who are extremely sensitive have had difficult relationships with authority figures in their youth. So it is important for them to have a nourishing relationship with the director. And the fastest way to achieve this is with "gratuitous" praise. When I say gratuitous praise, I mean not waiting for the actor to do something noticeably admirable. Praise whatever is there. Whatever is there is praiseworthy.

The artist is a person whose business in life is to praise. Artists discover the wonders of nature and we call attention to those wonders. The theatre artist gathers people into a dark room and says to them, "Look what we've discovered. Isn't this admirable? Isn't this wonderful? Isn't this awesome? Isn't this amazing?" An artist is someone who draws attention to what is praiseworthy in the Universe.

A director must be skilled in finding what is praiseworthy in nature because he is awakening the wonder and admiration of the actor as well as the audience. It is his business to draw attention to the wonder of things, the beauty of things, the peculiarity of things, the humor and wit of things, the irony of things, the joy of things, the awe of things, the uncertainty of things, the admirability of things. The director is a person whose job is to seek constantly what is wonderful in nature, and to awaken wonder in other people. In that sense, the director must be very disciplined. He goes around extracting from nature what is beautiful and revealing it to others. A director is not allowed the luxury of merely riding on the bus like everyone else. A director is a person who, by definition, is in quest of what is admirable or awesome in nature; who, by compulsion, cannot help but seek opportunities to draw the attention of others to that beauty and that wonder.

Now, habitual admiration is not usually a natural tendency. Most directors have to develop the technique. We learn by praising things unreasonably. We abandon our critical faculties for a time. We praise first and figure out why afterward. "Oh, what a beautiful yellow flower. It is so sunny." The quality of admirableness comes after the praise. It is a discipline. A director has to discipline himself in this. Part of our business is to promote awe, wonder, and admiration for the Universe. We cannot promote praise in others until we have practiced it ourselves and made it a habitual activity.

If you have difficulty finding something praiseworthy, imagine that it doesn't exist. One of my favorite expressions, and one that has pulled me out of many a difficulty, is this: "A thing becomes beautiful because of the possibility of its absence." I once heard of someone who said, "I was angry with you until it occurred to me that you might die before we settled our dispute. When I thought of you as dead, I lost my anger." When we imagine the absence of something, it becomes extremely beautiful.

One of the best examples of this is in *Our Town*. Emily has what might be called a commonplace admiration of life until she dies. Then in the third act, having died, she goes back to visit all those commonplace things that she took for granted—bacon frying in a pan, the smell of coffee. These commonplace things, which she had taken for granted, suddenly awaken tremendous admiration and love in her once she has been removed from them. A thing becomes beautiful because of the possibility of its absence, and if you have difficulty admiring something, imagine its nonexistence; it suddenly becomes incandescent, vibrant. It becomes emblazoned with a beauty you had not witnessed before.

The phrase "A thing becomes beautiful because of the possibility of its absence" is a lever that a director can use as a technique to increase his potential for praise. A director is a purveyor of praise. One of my favorite expressions is, "How beautiful that is." It is completely refreshing and it is a step up the ladder of wonder. If you have said how beautiful something is, the beauty of it will light up for you.

It is important for a director to practice praising. Begin the rehearsal with praise. "It is an honor to work with such fine artists." "This is one of the most beautiful plays ever written." "Look at the beautiful sunshine." "Aren't these words exciting. Let's begin." Your praise evokes enthusiasm, and the actor thinks, "Maybe he will praise me one day." He works in hope of being praised. Praise is the musculature of directing. All the theories and concepts can be thrown out the window; they are a dime a dozen. Any director who has a long career is a good praiser. You can practically measure a director's career by his enthusiasm for what he witnesses.

## BATTLES

From time to time, there may arise what might be called a battle between the director and an actor. What do you do? The director always surrenders. That is the law. The reason for this is practical. If you win a battle with an actor, you lose. There's no such thing as a director winning a battle with an actor. So, if the beginning of a battle occurs, you yield immediately. It doesn't make any difference what the issue is. "I absolutely refuse to wear those boots." "Well, let's find something else for you to wear. What would be better?" As soon as you accept a supportive position, the next step is creative.

If the director has an ego problem, it may be impossible for him to lose a battle with an actor. Then he must go back to grade one and become a stage manager until he has learned that his ego must be subservient to the art and that he must be graceful in relation to the actor. As we've said before, the director needs the actor as an ally, and we defeat our purpose completely if we make the actor an adversary. In battles, the director always loses.

## FORGIVENESS

It is a useful idea to encourage your actors to forgive themselves the minute something goes awry. No matter how clumsily something is done, you communicate to them, "Oh, never mind," or "That's all right," or as Tyrone Guthrie used to say, "Right! ON!" Teach the actors that self-forgiveness is an important technique. Harold Clurman used to say, "Forgive yourself as you go along." If you are too exacting of yourself, the work gets tied in knots and you never progress. You need to have a "cancel" technique that somewhat resembles the technique of a stand-up comic. When he fails to get a laugh, he mutters, "Yep, well, nothing!" and goes right on. Encourage instant self-forgiveness in actors.

## QUESTIONS FROM ACTORS

We've said before—but it's so important it bears repeating—a question from an actor is *not* a question. A question from an actor is an innocent bid to draw the director's attention to something unresolved. When the actor asks a question, a wise director doesn't answer the question. The answer to the question is not in the director; the answer to the question is in the actor. Answer the question by asking another question. Allow the actor to resolve the difficulty. He already has the best answer in mind before he asks the question. Here is an example:

ACTOR: Shall I wear this hat?
DIRECTOR: What would be best?
ACTOR: Well, it's too small. It gets in the way. I don't know where to put it, and if I do put it down, I have no way of getting it off stage when I leave.
DIRECTOR: Let's leave the hat out.

Another example:

ACTOR: How should I do it, on the right or the left?
DIRECTOR: Which way is best?
ACTOR: If I do it on the right, I can arrive on time. If I do it on the left, I'll be late.
DIRECTOR: Well, then do it on the right.

The answer to the question is in the question. The actor's answer will be organic, and by using his solution, the director will avoid imposing anything. Another example:

ACTOR: Are we going to skip this scene today?
DIRECTOR: Is there something about that scene that we should give our attention to?
ACTOR: Well, I did a lot of work on that scene last night and I have some new ideas I'd like to show you.
DIRECTOR: In that case, let's be sure to work that scene in.

The question "Are we going to skip this scene?" may be answered, "Yes, it's not scheduled!" or "Yes, we're moving on to the last act." But, "Are we going to skip this scene?" is an invitation to draw attention to something. The director does not know what it is; he has to find out. A question from the actor is merely an invitation. The actor is drawing attention to something unresolved.

## CHALLENGES AND OPPORTUNITIES

Just as a question is a signal to the director, so also the proposition of a "problem" is a signal. In the creative process, we don't recognize the existence of problems. We acknowledge them as challenges. We don't have trouble, we have opportunities. If you think you have a problem, then you consider yourself to be surrounded by confusion, and if you think yourself surrounded by confusion, you *are* surrounded by confusion.

In the creative process, we have a shift in thought. We no longer have problems, we have challenges. We no longer have troubles, we have opportunities. Every moment in the rehearsal where confusion or uncertainty or conflict arise must be immediately converted into an opportunity for creative adventure, or into a challenge to find appropriate solutions.

The director acknowledges the existence of a problem but converts it immediately into a challenge; then he asks for options and listens carefully. I suggest that this is the swiftest, most efficient, and least emotionally complicated method of working.

## QUESTIONS

A director thrives when he puts his ideas in the form of questions. You have known directors to come into rehearsal crying, "I want this. I want that. I see it this way. My entire concept. . . I need so many people on this side. I want you here. . . ." This is an amateur at work. He once overheard himself praised as being a director who "knows what he wants." He uses the rehearsal as an endless opportunity to tell everyone what he wants. He puts the word "I" at the beginning of all his sentences, which leads one to believe that he is living in an ego bind. A director in an ego bind should not be given the leadership of a group of creative actors. If he uses the word "I" recklessly and compulsively, the likelihood is that he is untrustworthy. A skilled director's sentences are questions. "How could we improve this? How could we clarify this? How could we get across the idea that she is looking for help? How could we simplify this entrance? Where has he come from? What does she have in mind? What is the objective in this scene? Could we try this again? Could we upgrade the objective? Could we pick up the pace?" When the director limits himself as much as possible to asking questions, the actor develops a habit of right answers. The encouraged actor rapidly develops intuitive right knowledge. His answers become more sure and true the longer you rehearse, because the actor learns to leave his intellect—the left-brain, critical faculties—and his ego-testing games behind. Soon the actor develops the characteristic of perpetual intuitive right thought. Ask an actor a question and have implicit trust in his intuitive right thought.

In this way, a director saves a great deal of time, and he does not have to think up all the answers himself. You have the actors to provide the answers, and you know they will be right.

It is an illusion for a director to believe that everything depends on his having figured out everything in advance. Not only is this impossible, but the notion introduces great stress into the rehearsal process. If the director had to figure out all the details for all the actors, he would fret sleeplessly every night of the rehearsal period—wakened by nightmares of an endless parade of decisions to be made. Then he would come into rehearsals grumpy, confused, and defensive, trying to impose unilateral and nonorganic directives upon a cast already prepared to unleash their own intuitive right knowledge into the situation. He only frustrates them. He blocks the path of creative flow by forcing his own ideas, his own solutions, and his own decisions, when he should be inviting their creative suggestions. It is preferable for a director to do his "creative homework"—and then abandon it and ask the actors questions.

## "COULD I TALK TO YOU ABOUT MY PART?"

This question represents a signal to the director, and he must be sensitive to the message. Many actors ask the question during the rehearsal process. At the moment an actor says, "Could I talk to you about my part?" the director must become super-sensitive. He must stop doing whatever he is doing and give the actor his full attention. That sentence carries the actor's message of ultimate urgency. He must hear good news from the director at that moment, and he must have the director's full attention. If possible talk to him right away, at least to find out what the key to his discomfort is. The actor must get an answer that tells him that he is going to have an opportunity for an intimate and complete discussion with the director alone. It's better not to postpone it. The director sets a time and place where there will be no distractions. There should be no other actor within hearing and sometimes even no stage managers. The question is really not a request to talk about the part. The question is usually an indication that the actor needs to be told that he's on the right track. He cannot go a step further without the assurance that what he's doing is okay. Sometimes it is possible to say simply, "You're doing a beautiful job and I'm thrilled with the way it's going. Keep working the way you're going. It's coming nicely." The actor may be quite satisfied with this. But perhaps there is someone or something that is really troubling the actor. He must have the opportunity to receive your exclusive attention.

His difficulty may come in all sorts of disguises. It may be that one of the other actors is giving him some trouble. Perhaps he feels awkward about a certain scene or a certain kiss, or about his appearance, or about a certain emotional response. The minute you hear that question, it is very important that you give it your immediate and full attention. Don't let it slip by, because the actor could be very upset at that moment; if you don't catch him, pull him up, and resolve his difficulty then and there, he may slide over into dejection or resentment. It's much more difficult to pull him out of that. If he grows morose and inefficient, it's because he didn't receive an answer when he asked, "Could I talk with you about my part?"

Many directors enjoy having private meetings with their actors. "Let's talk about it over lunch." I'm not really big on that sort of thing. I do, however, try to have a short, private conversation with each actor about his character sometime within the first week of rehearsal.

## WHAT DO YOU DO WHEN AN ACTOR AVOIDS THE EMOTIONAL CONTENT?

I once worked with an extremely talented actor who was very guarded in the part of Andre in *The Three Sisters*. We had already done three or four runthroughs of the play; one day we had just finished running the third act. I called a short break so that people could refresh themselves. The actor went into the hall. I followed him and when we were alone I said to him, "How long have I known you?" He said, "Sixteen years." I said,

"We went to school together, we acted together, we performed in many plays together. As you are playing this scene in the third act, you are hiding from the experience. Now it's time to suffer. It's time to pull out the stops and let yourself experience the scene. You can't delay it any longer. It is necessary. It's required by the play. I've known you too long to let you walk through it in this way. Now is the time. Do it." We went back to rehearsal. No one else in the company knew I had spoken to him. I said, "We'll take the third act again." It came time for his big scene at the end of the act and he tore the walls down. His dark glasses flew off as he cried, "For God's sake, see me as I am." He fulfilled the scene. We wept. The other actors wept. At the end of the act everyone fell into embraces. Sometimes an actor needs to be pushed. But one must be very sensitive to the timing and the wording.

## WHAT IF THE ACTOR IS RELYING ON OLD TRICKS TO AVOID DIRECT CONTACT WITH THE ROLE?

You could say, "Listen, your work has always been very *safe* in this area. Why don't you try something really splashy here for a change? I want you to go all the way with something new," or "You've never used this approach before. Let's try it together. If it doesn't work, you can always take the conventional approach," or "You know certain directors have called your attention to a problem or a mannerism in your work. Why don't we give that our complete attention in this rehearsal and master it? Why don't we explore that aspect completely in this production so that it never bothers you again?"

I worked with a very good actor once whose work was almost completely convincing, but as he acted he revealed traces of what appeared to be an attitude of obedience. It was as if an occasional inner voice was asking, "Did I get that right?" I drew his attention to this tendency and suggested, "Let's use this rehearsal period to get rid of this aspect of obedience. I want you to own your own territory, possess your own actions, and assert yourself completely. Dismiss that authority who is sitting in the back of your brain telling you to be obedient." The actor enjoyed that. As the rehearsal progressed the actor would check with me: "Did I own my territory today?" Gradually he overcame the trait and nowadays he acts with tremendous authority.

## INTELLECT

Talking, theorizing, and intellectualizing must be reduced to an absolute minimum. A good director does not enter into intellectual disputations over the play or the characters. Such emphasis on rationality abruptly shifts the creative process into the left brain. It misleads the actors into thinking that they can make points by using their intellects. Never allow an actor to entangle you in intellectuality. The way to avoid it is to assume an appearance of vagueness. Seem unqualified to enter that realm and say, "Yes, Yes. Well, when we get into rehearsal, show me. Let me see it. Show it to me. I'm sure it is all very good." Most discussion is fruitless.

## OPINION AND COMPLAINT

In the theatre, everyone considers himself an expert. The critics speak from a position of assumed omnipotence, and every member of the audience fashions himself an expert, not only at playwriting but at acting and directing as well. This brings to mind the famous adage about opinions: They are like a nether part of the anatomy of which everybody has one. A professional director is one who has disciplined his tendency to elaborate on personal opinions. Everyone has an opinion. The parading of opinions is frequently an ego-opportunity for an individual to upgrade his self-esteem when he is in the company of impressionables.

As for complaining, it is opposite to the artist's disposition. An artist is a person who uses whatever is given in a creative manner. To complain that the production would have been better if there had been more rehearsal is simply to say what every director always feels. There is never enough rehearsal. There is never enough money. There is never enough time. To complain merely gives evidence of amateur status. A professional uses what is given to him. He neither apologizes for his work nor complains about the circumstances, unless, of course, he intends to change them and do something about them; that is not complaint but a statement of creative resolution.

## TOUCHING

A wise director touches. In Europe, the moment the director enters the room, he goes around to each individual in the room and gives a very quick little handshake. The rehearsal does not begin until he has touched everyone in the room.

A recent experiment took place in a bank. One week the teller touched the people, brushed their fingers lightly as she handed them their money. The following week she was careful to avoid physical contact while passing the money. The customers were polled after leaving the bank. In the first week, the people who had received the brushing contact evaluated the bank as trustworthy, efficient, reliable, friendly, cooperative. In the second week the people who had not been touched found the bank to be unreliable, sloppy, unfriendly, and even suspect.

Certain tests with monkeys have proved that a touch carries with it a profound message. Monkeys that have not been touched often enough in youth develop antisocial behavior—schizophrenia, deep withdrawal, depression, inordinate fears, and hostility.

A handshake is a conventional formality that contains an opportunity to touch someone. One of the reasons the custom of touching the hands has evolved is that the hand is generally considered for use and is a neutral part of the body. Some individuals feel frightened if they are touched on the chest, on the waist, or on the thigh. If a person in a position of authority touches on the thigh, it could lead to confusion in the mind of the one who is touched. If a person in authority touches an individual on the top of the head, it has a very significant connotation, almost like a blessing. If a person in authority touches someone on the cheek or neck, another message is communicated. If a person in authority touches someone on the forehead, there is another message. Touching someone just under the crook of the elbow is a message of helpfulness and support. Touching on the forearm, especially on the top of the forearm, is another message. Placing your hand on top of another person's hand is another message. When a person in authority touches an individual on the knee, it is an extremely intimate touch but a very friendly one. Touching someone on the foot has a very funny message—playful and innocent. Touching carries a wide variety of messages; the director learns to use those messages effectively, because the message in one touch is swift, efficient, clear. At the end of rehearsal one frequently does not have time to compliment each actor on his work that day, but one can usually stand between them and the door and touch them, each one, just lightly before they leave. You do not need to say anything to them. I hug them. It may be indiscriminate, but the message is complete.

## SCHEDULING REHEARSAL

Always begin rehearsal on time. There are some directors who like to gossip and joke and waste the first ten or twelve minutes. This awakens a sense of sloppiness in the actor and gives him the feeling that the work is not important. If he takes his role seriously, he is likely to resent any waste of the rehearsal time. Always start precisely on time. On the other hand, if there is an actor who is late for the first few times, let it pass unnoticed. It is better not to say, "Why are you seven minutes late?" That's unnecessary. If an actor is late, simply begin rehearsing without him; when he arrives he will understand that he is expected to be there on time.

I always stop work at the precise moment indicated on the schedule. I ask the stage manager to give me a signal seven minutes before the scheduled end to give us time for a few quick notes after running the scene through once without stopping.

Going overtime on rehearsal is disrespectful of the actors, who have made plans to be elsewhere. Resentment and noncreativity pile up rapidly for every minute the director tries to rehearse after the deadline.

In scheduling a rehearsal, there are two procedures that are usually practiced. Some directors call the entire cast and have them wait in a side room all day while they work with whomever they may need. Occasionally, of course, this procedure cannot be avoided, but as a general procedure, this practice is debilitating and wasteful. It is a dishonor to the actors to treat them as if they are in service to the director—as if the director can pick them up and fling them back whenever he needs them. In addition, it wears the actor out. While an actor waits in an anteroom, he rarely works on his script. Actors are more likely to work on a crossword puzzle; to gossip, take naps, eat too much, or hang around and get bored. By the time they are called to rehearse, they are fatigued and their attitude is uncooperative because they have wasted so much time. They may be resentful at having waited so long while the director indulged himself at their expense.

The other procedure—the method I subscribe to—is for the director to estimate how long he wants to work on a certain scene and to call only those actors needed for that particular scene. For a beginning director it may be difficult to estimate the time needed for each scene. When in doubt, estimate that a four-page scene will take one hour and fifteen minutes. Only call those actors needed for that scene. The actors appreciate this because it allows them to plan their lives more effectively. They will do better homework on their roles and they will come in better prepared.

## ATTENTION SPAN

Knowledge of and respect for the attention span is pertinent to the success of the rehearsal. Tests have shown that the average adult mind, especially when involved in creative work, can concentrate on one thing for fifty-five to seventy-five minutes.

The downward curve of effectiveness after one hour and fifteen minutes is very rapid. After about seventy-five minutes, one suddenly begins to experience an avalanche of ineffective thought—false starts, confusion, mistakes, boredom, uncertainty, needless repetition, disorientation. It is important for a director to know this. I have seen directors work on one scene for five hours straight. This is unnatural and nature will kick back at them, causing inefficiency, confusion, frustration, and disharmony. It is practical for a director to change the subject of an actor's attention every seventy minutes. Frequently, it is a good idea to rehearse a new group of actors who are fresh. But if the play requires you to continue with one group, take a short recess and proceed to a new scene.

## LEARNING PROCESS

Now, during the process of rehearsing the scene, how do we apportion the time? Our knowledge of the nature of the learning process gives us the answer. We have said before that the learning process is divided into three steps. The first step of the learning process is the *discovery,* the second step is the *test,* and the third step is the *pattern-set.* Essentially, a rehearsal period is a learning period, in that the actors are learning how the play goes, learning what the performance will be like.

Let's divide our seventy-minute rehearsal into three segments, not necessarily of equal length, and say that the first segment will be the time allocated for discovery, the second period will be for testing, and the third period will be for setting the pattern. Having said this, I will now describe what I do when I call a scene to rehearse.

If I plan to rehearse for seventy minutes on one scene, I first ask the actors to run through the scene without stopping. This is the discovery phase. I want them to discover (1) new things about the scene, (2) the accumulated effect of previous work on the scene, (3) the effect of their recent homework, and (4) the effect of the time lapse since the last rehearsal—the subconscious mind will have added new colors. I also want them to rediscover the sounds of their own voices at this particular time.

The first part of the rehearsal, then, is a discovery. I allow the actors to do the entire scene without interruption, because to interrupt them would make discovery impossible. This period is also a discovery period for the director. He is discovering how far his team has progressed since the last rehearsal and whether he has made the right choices. He is discovering whether the actor is on the beam, whether the actor has done any homework, and whether anything has been overlooked. The director is discovering new intuitive responses that awaken new creative ideas in his own mind. It is very important that the first time through there be no interruptions.

The second phase is the testing phase. We could also call this the working phase. You take the scene and go through it slowly, bit by bit, making suggestions, asking questions, trying the business one way and then another, working your way gradually through the scene—only once, but very slowly. This is the longest segment of the rehearsal process. During this phase you never go back to the beginning and start over. You just work through patiently, two or three lines at a time, on to the next piece of business and the next and so forth. But you never say, "Let's take it from the beginning." You work steadily and gradually, section by section, through the entire scene. This gives you and the actors the opportunity to clarify difficulties and to test values and the various possibilities. I always try to terminate the testing phase at least seven minutes before rehearsal is scheduled to end, even if I haven't completed the work I had planned to do. I call off the "workthrough" and simply say, "Now it is time to put the pieces together and see what we have done."

Now we go into the third phase of the learning process, which is the pattern-set. "Let's begin at the beginning of the scene," I say, "and go through to the end, and—this is absolutely essential—we won't stop, no matter what happens. I may have a few comments at the end." Now I let them run it through no matter how terrible the form may be. Once again, I stress that at this point the director does not interrupt, because the actors are in the process of setting the pattern. They must be allowed to set the pattern, no matter how rough, no matter how incomplete, no matter how confused the work may seem to be. This gives the actors a sense of achievement and self-respect. It shows them how much progress has been made and how much closer they have come to the realization of the inner life. At the end of this little runthrough, the director retains a few moments to make suggestions—one or two notes and a little congratulation. "Yes, it's coming nicely. Keep on working. I'll see you tomorrow."

You see what a formal pattern I impose on the rehearsal process. This pattern is based on a knowledge of the learning process and of the attention span. Any more work would be nonproductive. If you work them any longer, their attention will decline; distractions and mistakes will creep in, and success will diminish rapidly. The learning process has been completed. Having divided our one hour and ten minutes into phases of discovering, testing, and pattern-setting, we leave it alone and go on to something new.

## INTERRUPTION

One of the most important things a director can learn is how *not* to interrupt. The director doesn't have to be an intellect or a zealot, but he must be self-disciplined. He must know what not to do. To interrupt is rude. To interrupt someone who is trying to express himself is unforgivable. It doesn't make any difference what he is saying. Anyone who makes a practice of interrupting is revealing himself to be ill bred, selfish, and irresponsible. For a director to interrupt an actor while he is acting is even more reprehensible, because the actor, as a good director knows, has to shift gears in order to begin again. He has to "get into it" again. The process of getting into it may seem to be a very tiny shift in the actor's mental position. That transition takes place in a mere matter of seconds, and in the theatre we are used to it; but it is frequently a big internal leap into the inner life of the character.

Now, when a director repeatedly interrupts, stopping and

starting, the most indescribable frustration builds up in the actor. Indeed, the resentment and rage may accumulate to such a point that the actor is unable to think or act clearly. I have seen actors under such pressure start to shake; their eyes bulge; they stomp about, mimic the director, tear their hair, gasp, snort, tremble, growl, and spit. If an actor learns that a director is an interrupter, the actor dreads going into rehearsal. He feels that at any moment someone may chop off his fingers. The actor will gradually become so frustrated and uptight that he will be unable to rehearse. The likelihood is that he will stop speaking to the director or will fly into a rage over some small point, leaving the director to wonder what the difficulty was. The actor discovers he abhors rehearsing with that director, even though he may be unable to explain why.

There are two ways a director can avoid interrupting his actors. If the rehearsal scene is short, he can simply remember the things that went wrong and mention them to the actors after the scene has been completed. Or, if he has a poor memory, he can jot little notes and pass them on to the actors after the scene. The acting process is sacred, and in the rehearsal room the acting process is being born. The process is very sensitive. A director who interrupts on a habitual basis is essentially badgering the actor, and that badgering will be retaliated in some form of revenge. Such a director lacks self-discipline and respect for the actor and is courting trouble in the form of an explosion.

Even in the second phase of the rehearsal process, the testing phase, the skilled director does not interrupt very much. He'll say, "Let's take the next five lines," and then work the next five lines. Then he says, "Now, let's work it up to Sarah's entrance," and the actors do that section; "Let's take from here to the exit," and together they work over each section three or four times. But it is helpful not to interrupt even a little section. Better to play it through, make suggestions, then play it through again. Don't interrupt in the middle.

Some directors, for lack of experience, have a bad habit of going back to the beginning and starting again, so that the first eight lines of the scene are over-rehearsed and the last three lines of the scene are never spoken. One must get out of the habit of saying, "Let's take it from the top." It is a good idea in the work phase of the rehearsal to have the stage manager feed the actor the lines you desire for the pickup. Don't let the actors say, "Let's pick it up from where I say . . ." or "Why don't you feed me the line about . . . ?" Turn to the stage manager and say, "Give them a line at . . ." and let the stage manager tell the actor where to pick it up. If you leave it to the actors, they will go back three pages.

## "LET ME SHOW YOU" AND LINE-READINGS

There are a pair of rules that go together. The first is: Never do the actions for the actors. Never say, "Let me show you how I want it." Never put yourself into the actor's place and never illustrate the result for him. Suggest it, coax it, cartoon it, but never *do* it for the actor. The resentment that is caused in the actor by such usurpation can never be recovered. Stand on your head to *elicit* that action you seek, but never actually do it.

The second rule, a corollary to the first, is: Never read the line for the actor. Never even speak the line that the actor has to speak. That is his line. The director must never say those words.

If you want an actor to give a certain reading, there are techniques for eliciting the reading you want. Use the phrase "operative word" and say, "I think such and such is the operative word and the rest is all thrown away," or "Please feature this word," or "Frame this idea," or "This phrase is difficult for the audience to understand." In this way the actor will usually agree to try new readings, but at least you have left the line in his mouth—you have not *said* the line for him. Another method is to paraphrase the line, giving it the precise expression that you are seeking, but still avoiding the actual use of his words. Occasionally, in desperate moments, I will even whistle the tune of the line—the desired vocal inflection. Whistle it. Sing it. Paraphrase it. Describe it. But the actor is the only one permitted to speak his lines. For directors, line-readings are forbidden.

## ENCOURAGEMENT

I observed Francis Ford Coppola use a wonderful technique when he was working on a production of *Private Lives*. He never told the actors what *not* to do. He would do a scene again and again, and each time he would say to the actor, "What you did at that moment—I *liked* that. And where you came in and approached her, I *liked* what happened there. More of that! And where you were trying to make her answer you—I *liked* that, more of that!" He would tell them what he liked and encourage them to do "more." He never told them they were doing something wrong.

Actors come from families in which their parents were probably telling them that they did everything wrong. Almost all actors could do no right for their parents. So it is not a creative situation if the director, in a parental or authoritarian role, is constantly telling the actor that he's doing something wrong. It is, in fact, the worst relationship a director can have with an actor: the punitive parent, the scolded child. A rehearsal under such conditions is painful. An actor *wants* to do it right. All he needs is to be freed and encouraged with occasional guidance.

## REHEARSING ALONE

Some directors love to say to actors, "Why don't you all get together and go into a room someplace and work this all out and bring it in and show me tomorrow." This approach should be forbidden. I never allow even two actors to work together alone without my being in the room. The reason for this is that when two actors are left alone together without a monitor, one actor invariably places himself above the other actor. If they are left alone, there will be a little light conversation, a slight jockeying, a few moments of testing, and suddenly, automatically and unconsciously, one of them comes out on top. In no time, he expands that position until soon he's giving instructions to the other actor. The other actor, although silent, resents all this and feels, "Why am I being pushed into a position of subservience to someone I am expected to share the stage with?" You may rehearse with them for another three weeks, but the fact that one of them won the upper hand and the other became subservient will mar their relationship during the rehearsal of that play. Nothing you can do will remedy the situation once they have had this little contest of who is on top and who is subservient. An experienced director seldom sends actors off to rehearse by themselves.

Of course, now and then there is an exception. When there is not enough rehearsal time, you may occasionally send a couple of experienced, evenly matched actors to rehearse alone, but you give them instructions in advance and you send a stage manager with them. My instruction to the stage manager would be, "Permit no discussion of the scene. Just run the scene three or four times, but do not let the actors enter into any discussion of the merits of the scene, the blocking, the business, meaning, or interpretation."

From time to time actors will ask, "Is it okay if we get together on our own to run lines?" I will occasionally consent if the actors are evenly matched and I am very sure of them, but only after giving them a short lecture. At this moment, I take on the bearing of a stern parent, even to the inclusion of a wagging finger. "But you both must *promise me* . . . (pause for emphasis) . . . promise me to run the lines three times and that there will be no . . . (pause, with a repeat for emphasis) . . . no discussions of the scene. Just a line rehearsal. Do you *promise?*" Having extracted an absolute promise, I send them off. By my imposing strict conditions on their rehearsal together, it would be difficult for either to drift into a manipulative position.

Even with the finest, most experienced actors, one of them might ever so casually drop a remark like, "You know when you say that line? It would be so helpful if you would just point the last word." The minute one actor has made a request of that sort without the director being present, he has taken the upper position and the other actor is down. The ensuing resentment is nearly irreversible.

Never allow an actor to assume a more elevated position than his fellow actor. Each actor is counting on the director to keep fairness in the work. Each actor plays *his own part*.

## DISCUSSION BETWEEN ACTORS

In the rehearsal, I never permit an actor to tell another actor how to do something. Never. If I find an actor making a suggestion to another actor, I immediately say, "When you have an idea, please tell me. If you'd like another actor to do something that would be helpful to you, ask me. I will be glad to pass it on." I always pass it on, but I pass it on as my own suggestion, in my own words. I don't say, "So and so would like you to stand . . ." I pass it on as my own idea. If the suggestion is not a helpful one, I ask whoever made it to "hold on to that idea for a few days and I will see what I can do about it." By postponing, the bad idea frequently falls out of orbit naturally.

## OPEN REHEARSAL

There is an old Russian proverb: Never show unfinished work to a child or a fool. Do not allow anyone to watch a rehearsal who may later come to the actor and give advice on his performance. If your stage managers are not absolutely professional, be sure to say to them, "I prohibit all outside discussion of the play or characters with the actors," so that the stage managers are forewarned that they must never discuss the work with the actors. Nor do we permit one actor to consult with another actor for advice. This is unprofessional. It is important that until the play opens the actor receives his creative guidance from one source. I definitely discourage actors from having sideline coaching sessions with other actors; or with playwrights—whom

I would forbid even to *speak* with an actor except in my presence—agents, wives, husbands, friends, or passing admirers. The growth of a performance is so subtle and so special that one sentence, one ill-chosen phrase, is capable of throwing an actor into labyrinths of wrong thought. Of course, the young or unskilled actor will call this bosh, but an experienced actor knows how true it is.

There is another situation that arises frequently in New York when, at the first preview, everyone's agent shows up. After the performance, the agent will invariably tell the client what is wrong with everybody else's performance and how everyone on the stage is ruining the client's performance. "So and so is upstaging you. So and so is trying to steal your best scene. . . . So and so is an awful actor. You would be much better if you had a different dress and came on earlier. You really need another scene to explain your part." As director I always gather the actors together the day before all those influential people are about to descend and make their mark. I say, "For four weeks we have worked to create one united and harmonic picture. Now we are all going to hear other people's impressions. I hope you will keep your eyes on your goal. I don't want to take out a lot of 'improvements' after the next performance." If you have had harmonic rehearsals for four weeks, the actors trust you more than they are apt to trust the comments of their wives or agents.

## SCAPEGOATISM

Some directors cannot help but use a strange mode of scapegoatism; it is a deadly characteristic. If you find you have a tendency toward it, get rid of it. It will destroy every production that you work on, and it will ruin your reputation. Scapegoatism represents the case of a director who has the illusion that all his problems are caused by one member of the company; that "if it weren't for that one," the production would be wonderful. A director who vents his irritations on one particular actor should be publicly exposed. The other actors should drive the director out of the theatre. That scapegoatism should happen in professional theatre is shocking, because it means that the professional director simply doesn't understand one of his principal responsibilities—to unite the actors under his care.

Many directors have never suffered the confusion and humiliation that most actors have suffered in the attempt to create a performance. That is a pity. All directors, in my opinion, should have to act. When you act, you find out how painful it is to have the disapproval of your director. You learn how awful it is to go home night after night knowing that the only acknowledgement the director has given you has been a sneer as you walked off stage or a tired glance to heaven when your name was mentioned. The actor goes home and dies a thousand deaths. The slightest rejection from the director during the rehearsal process can cause tremendous depression for the actor. Now if as the director you cause that depression, you are going to have to live with the results—less creativity, less spontaneity, and less success for the play and for everyone involved with it.

It is very important never to say or do anything that will lessen the actor's sense of well-being. Immediately after his sense of well-being is wounded, he becomes less creative. It is important at the end of each rehearsal to give every actor the message that what he has done that day was constructive. As a skilled director, you learn to send these messages in very short forms. "Good work today" can be said to the entire cast at the end of the scene. To the actor this means that once again he can go home peacefully, study his lines, and feel confident in his work.

## DEPERSONALIZED DIRECTION

In presenting his ideas to the cast, it is critical for the director to avoid any possibility of an ego conflict. To this end, it is helpful if he chooses to present his ideas in a nonpersonal way.

There are directors who stand in the center of the rehearsal floor repeatedly using phrases such as, "I want you here," and "I want you there," and "I want you to come in very fast," and "Now I want you to take it again." By the frequent use of the word "I," the director invites the actor to take a similar position; the possibility for a conflict arises when the actor says, "I want to go into the center." The director answers by saying, "I want you back on the side."

The rehearsal flows much more freely if the director allows the process to develop on the basis of the needs of the script and the needs of the other actors. A director working in this way would be inclined to use remarks such as, "This play needs great clarity of speech," or "This scene allows you to go all the way here," or "It wants a big protest from you," or "Let's see what happens if we have you in the center for this," or "How would it be if you came in from the side?" These suggestions all lack the prefix of ego. They make it much easier for an actor to feel that the director is working with him and not using him.

## OFFSTAGE RELATIONSHIPS

It will happen from time to time that the actor playing Romeo will persuade himself that the most creative use of his time is to have a love affair with the actress playing Juliet. It is imagined that this intimacy will improve the performance. In all of its various guises, such a postulation is false. For the record, it must be said squarely that the best relationship between a pair of onstage lovers is a remote and professional relationship offstage. I would actively try to dissuade the leading lady and the leading man from courting during the rehearsal period. After the opening of the production, what they do is their own business.

Occasionally what happens is that the leading lady and leading man decide to go to bed after the third day of rehearsal. By the fourth day of rehearsal, their illusions are shattered. Either they are unable to speak to each other, or one has so deeply offended the other that they find it impossible to act together. Try whenever possible to have the leading actors postpone their amorous adventures until after the opening. It will be good for both of them, and it will be good for the success of the production.

# Objectives

## THE GOLDEN KEY

In the empty space before us there is a chair. Let us say the chair is an ordinary household chair—straight backed, wooden, and green. Now, in our imaginations we place someone in the chair. This is the beginning of acting. The someone we place in the chair will be the character that we wish to portray. We can visualize him sitting there. We can sense him. We can smell him. We can hear his movements—for the purpose of this exercise, I'm going to use "he" or "his." Suffice it to say, the person in the chair could be a male or female.

The actor's purpose is, first, to observe the model in the chair and then to go sit inside the skin of the person in the chair. Before the actor goes and sits in the chair, he must *observe* the person in the chair with methodic scrutiny. When the character in the chair has been observed completely, the actor assumes the skin, contour, and personality of the character in the chair, as if stepping into the model's space, or sliding into an invisible envelope.

Let us look for a few moments at this character sitting before us. What is there about him that interests us? What could move us to imitate him? Let us list those aspects that fascinate us:

70

| | |
|---|---|
| his appearance | his hobbies |
| his movements | his social status |
| his smell | his politics |
| his nationality | his accomplishments |
| his habits | his attitude toward death |
| his memories | his family |
| his laugh | his friends |
| his failures | his religion |
| his dreams | his passions |
| his daydreams | his intellect |
| his nervous gestures | his education |
| his smile | his language |
| his mannerisms | his voice |
| his health | his posture |
| his loneliness | his weight |
| his age | his strengths |
| his fears | his diet |
| his weaknesses | his goals |
| his biography | his energy level |
| his needs | his likes and dislikes |
| his experiences | his sexuality |
| his wants | his eccentricities |
| his clothing | his sense of humor |
| his income | his temper |
| his birth sign | his pride or lack of it |
| his perceptions | his morality |
| his name | his self-confidence |
| his profession | his love |

We could add more; when the list was complete, we would have a fair and accurate picture of his character.

His name is Leslie. There he sits, gazing and breathing silently and motionlessly in the green chair before us; sitting there in his own clothing, in his own posture, in his own complexion, in his own thought, and in his own history.

I am the actor. I stand before Leslie observing him. He the

model, I the artist. I am to become him. I am to think his thoughts, share his feelings, speak his words. How shall I become him? He awes me. In some ways he and I are alike. But in most of the patterns of his life—his expressions, his rhythms, his looks, his wants, his background, his ways of going about things—he is very different from me. Yet to succeed I must believe myself to be him. His goals must become my goals. His appearance must become mine. His words must rise from my heart and soul, and I must experience his pain.

My model slips a hand into his pocket as he turns his head slowly to look at me. How shall I become him? Where shall I begin? What path shall I use by which to enter his being? What shall I give my attention to first? Shall I study the entire history of his life? Shall I scrutinize his anatomy, his health, his diet, his grooming habits, his weight, his movements? Shall I begin by reconstructing his thought, his education, his self-discipline, his ethics, his I.Q., his confidence, his social position, his job, or his personal habits? I am beginning to sense that I could observe my model for years before I would be truly able to enter and become him, before I would be able to take on the heart of his unique and wonderful mystery. I sense the need for a technique, a shortcut, a device for entering him quickly, accurately, effortlessly. I need a *golden key*.

Let's look at Leslie again for a minute. Is he a happy man? Has he succeeded in everything he pursued? Is he in pain? Is he alone? Is he uncertain? Does he suffer? Does he think well of himself? Does he fear us? What part of himself does he seek to hide from scrutiny? See how he shifts his weight in the chair now that he knows we are looking at him. He raises one hand, presses his nostrils together lightly, looks at his shoe, curls his fingers, and places his fist behind his lower back.

There's no part of Leslie that is not going to be known to me. In time, I, as actor, am going to enter into Leslie. His life will be mine. I am going to borrow, for a prolonged period of time, his thoughts, his fears, his loves, and his desires. I am going to borrow the hair that grows out of his nostrils. I am going to borrow his central nervous system. I am going to borrow the story of his experience. I am going to borrow his mentality, his awareness, his pleasure. I am going to borrow his sense of humor. I'm going to borrow his rhythms. I'm going to borrow the pair of shoes he is wearing. But where shall I begin? Where is my golden key?

I return to the model. I study the model. I will give Leslie no rest until I have observed him completely. I will not rest until I have scanned and memorized everything about him. I will watch my model night and day. He will never be out of my presence. He will yield to me all his secrets.

I will walk around him for hours. I will pester him with questions. I will be exacting in detail. This is the first step in the acting process. I study the model:

> Leslie, where did you get that coat? What is in your pockets? Where did the smudge on your collar come from? Do you have callouses, freckles, corns? Do you have any scars? Have you ever had an operation? Ether? Flowers afterwards? From whom? When do you feel most lonely, Leslie? Whom do you love? Leslie! What are you thinking at this moment? Who is your favorite playmate? What foods give you heartburn? Can you keep a secret? Do you owe anyone money? What makes you laugh? Do you complain? Do you pray? Do you masturbate? What do you feel most lost without? Do you drink? Do you daydream? Do you worry? What, Leslie, is your absolutely most favorite thing in the world? What do you do in secret that no one is aware of? Tell me. How did your spinal column get the way it is? What is your strongest childhood memory? What is your pet peeve? What pain do you have in your body right now? Is there anything or anyone you hate? Is there a supreme being for you? Whom do you imitate?

As the actor, I study the model. I move around him steadily. Gradually, systematically, relentlessly, courageously I persuade him to yield up his truth to me; his heart, his being. Only when I know him thoroughly can I become him. Only when I share his thoughts, his hopes, his dreams will I be permitted to go and sit in the green chair in his place; only when I love him will he allow me to slide into his skin. The actor studies the model. This is the first step. But where is the golden key?

When the golden key is mine, then I will go to him, sit in his place, and become him. Then I will place my feet where his feet are. I will place my knees where his knees are, and my hands where his hands are. I will assume his carriage, his gait, his glance. I will take upon myself his mentality, his pain, his memory, his loneliness. I will take his voice. I will like what he likes. I will laugh at what amuses him. What he finds sexy will turn me on. What he has achieved will make me proud, and what he resents will make me indignant. His convictions will be my principles. I will consent to take onto myself all his life. When I agree to take on his life, I may be taking on a lot of weight, a lot of sorrow, a lot of suffering, a lot of resentment, a lot of fear, a lot of loneliness—all strange to my usual nature. I may take on ugliness, despair, bigotry, uncertainty, ill-fortune. But when I enter him I will include all, and I will dare to accept the entirety of his being. I will *become* Leslie.

The enormity of the task seems to be awesome. We have asked so many questions and received so many impressions. The sheer number of facets of Leslie's life and experience cause us to seek a simple, sure, and effortless method of becoming the character. We do not want to spend countless and unsystematic hours asking random questions and patching our haphazard impressions together in the hope that some accident will ignite a coherent and truthful performance. We need the golden key. We need a technique that will bring the multiplicity of impressions into alignment and unity.

Thanks to the methods articulated by our master, Constantin Stanislavski, we have a golden key. His study is a revelation to every serious actor.

Every skilled professional actor will be able to spot the golden key immediately in the following list of character traits. The golden key will leap out and light up as the one valuable tool for the actor; the other characteristics in the list will recede into the shadowy recess of secondary consideration. Can you spot the single golden key to which the actor should anchor his full attention from among the many we have discussed?

| | |
|---|---|
| his appearance | his religion |
| his loves | his use of language |
| his fears | his anger |
| his frustrations | his uncertainty |
| his nationality | his wants |
| his personal relations | his inner rage |
| his emotions | his ethics |
| his thoughts | his love |
| his habits | his loneliness |
| his memories | his pride |
| his sense of humor | his eccentricities |
| his childhood | his uniqueness |
| his daydreams | his education |
| his mannerisms | his awareness |
| his needs | his strengths |
| his hopes | his weaknesses |
| his physical health | his energy |
| his age | his mentality |
| his biography | his rhythms |
| his wardrobe | his sexuality |
| his birth sign | his expressions |
| his self-esteem | his habits |
| his social status | his pain |
| his profession | his mystery |
| his name | his pleasures |
| his hobbies | his central nervous system |
| his politics | his worries |

Did your eyes go right to the golden key? It may be correctly said that the actor is interested in every characteristic on the above list. But there is one particular word that is the tool, the lever, the power, the passion, the exercise, the obsession, the quest, the revelation, the liberator, and the joy of the genuine and knowledgeable actor. It is the golden key that frees all other creative energies. It is the golden key that unlocks and opens the gate, freeing my direct, clear, and easy path into the inner life of Leslie; so that I become him thoroughly, opulently, fearlessly, effortlessly. This technique is the key to all success in acting. This golden key is the sine qua non—or "without which nothing"—of the art of theatre. The professional actor could spot the golden key on that list from a mile away. The amateur is still puzzled. There is one and only one "open sesame" to creative acting. There is one and only one way to enter and know and experience and express the inner life of a character in a play. And that technique is the systematic and thorough pursuit of the *wants* of the character.

How simple it seems! How prosaic. How obvious. His *wants*. But the overwhelming majority of rehearsals are mired in confusion, frustration, and non-success, because the artists fix their attention on the secondary paraphernalia of results.

Wants. Wants. Wants. Wants are what create drama. Wants are what give life to the character. Wants are what the waking individual is never without. Wants are perpetual. Wants cause action. Wants create conflict. Wants are the very energy of human life and the *System of Wants* is the aspect of character to which the actor gives his relentless and obsessive attention. The actor tracks down the wants. Everything else is classified as a condition. The golden key is the character's system of wants. And after I have studied and structured and tested and *assumed* Leslie's system of wants, then, and only then, am I permitted to occupy his inner life and express his personality. Of all the questions I ask Leslie about himself, the overwhelming majority have to do with his wants: "What do you want?" "What do you want now?" "What is your ultimate want?" "What do you want from the other person?" "What do you want in the play?" "What do you want in life?" When I succeed in making Leslie's wants my wants, I succeed in the process of acting. The *want* is the golden key.

## A SYSTEM OF WANTS

I will want what Leslie wants.

It is essential at this point to divide wants into two classifications and to throw one of the classifications away.

Leslie may want a motorboat, a wife, a moment's peace and quiet. These are nouns.

In another category, Leslie may want to earn enough money to buy a motorboat; he may want to win Georgia's heart, to eliminate the distractions to his peace of mind. To earn, to win, to eliminate. These verbs are the wants.

We narrow the focus of the actor's pursuit now by stating clearly that, for our purposes in theatre, Leslie never wants nouns. His wants are expressed as verbs.

When asked what Leslie wants, a skilled actor will never answer that Leslie wants an object, or a person, or a job, or love, or independence. A skilled actor always states Leslie's wants in the form of a verb. What does Leslie want to *do?*

I WANT TO ___(verb)___ .

The behavior of an individual is caused by what he wants. What does Leslie want to *do?* What does he want to do for, or to, himself, and what does he want to do for, or to, other people? A serious actor doesn't give time or attention to any other aspect of the character until he has made a thorough study of what the character wants to do. Leslie is always wanting to do something. If he is awake he wants to do something to himself, to others, or to his surroundings. The one thing that is perpetual and constant in Leslie's consciousness is that he is always wanting. There is never a moment when a human being is not wanting to do something. Leslie may want to make himself more comfortable in his chair; he may want to convince me of his disinterest; he may want to get out of the room; he may want to fall asleep. He may want to figure out why I am gazing at him with such interest; but Leslie is always wanting to do something. He has many characteristics, but the one thing that he always has—if he is alive—is that he wants to do something. His entire life has been composed of a system of wants.

As an actor I say, "The only thing that interests me is what Leslie wants. I will study what he wants; when I know what he wants I will borrow his wants and make them my own. His wants will become my wants; and when I want completely what he wants, I will have entered the inner life of Leslie. Everything I do will flow from his nature."

The system of wants in Leslie is what the actor gives his absolute, continuous, and undivided attention to. The actor is like a detective hunting down those wants.

We have already narrowed our focus to eliminate nouns:

| NOUN | VERB |
| --- | --- |
| I want a motorboat. | I want to EARN enough for a motorboat. |
| I want a wife. | I want to WIN Georgia's heart. |
| I want peace. | I want to ELIMINATE distraction. |
| I want attention. | I want to FASCINATE everyone. |
| I want order. | I want to ORGANIZE this mess. |

Now let us narrow further and eliminate adjectives:

| ADJECTIVE | VERB |
| --- | --- |
| I am angry with her. | I want to DESTROY her. |
| I am nervous. | I want to FOCUS my attention. |
| I am frustrated. | I want to FIND a way out. |
| I am in love. | I want to TAKE CARE of her forever. |
| I am being charming. | I want to DAZZLE the guests. |
| I am confused. | I want to FIGURE OUT a solution. |
| I am giddy. | I want to CONTAIN my rapture. |
| I am drunk. | I want to PRESERVE business as usual. |
| I am friendly. | I want to WIN him over. |
| I am arrogant. | I want to BELITTLE him. |

Listed below are a number of frequently recurring "actable" verbs:

| | |
|---|---|
| I want to CONVINCE. | I want to HELP. |
| I want to ENCOURAGE. | I want to SEDUCE. |
| I want to PREPARE. | I want to IGNITE. |
| I want to ENLIGHTEN. | I want to BUILD. |
| I want to ANNIHILATE. | I want to HURT. |
| I want to GET EVEN. | I want to AWAKEN. |
| I want to OVERWHELM. | I want to MOCK. |
| I want to REASSURE | I want to CRUSH |
| I want to BOMBARD. | I want to INSPIRE. |
| I want to SUPPRESS. | I want to DESTROY. |
| I want to BELITTLE. | I want to INCITE. |
| I want to LAMBAST. | I want to TEASE. |

Having narrowed the focus of wants to the choice of specific verbs, let us take the first of two steps in refinement. An adequate expression of the want is a verb by itself. A superior, more subtle, and certainly more actable expression of the want will include the person to whom the want is directed and the response sought from that person, so that a first-class actor expressing an individual want of the character would include all three elements:

| | VERB | RECEIVER | DESIRED RESPONSE |
|---|---|---|---|
| I want .. | to WIN ......... | Gloria's ..... | admiration. |
| I want .. | to AWAKEN .... | my father's .. | enthusiasm. |
| I want .. | to REDUCE .... | my lover .... | to tears. |
| I want .. | to IGNITE ...... | the crowd ... | to riot. |
| I want .. | to PERSUADE .. | Ann ........ | to kiss me. |

This is the most sophisticated and effective expression of Leslie's wants because it includes the other person's response. This three-part mechanism requires Leslie to be *dependent* on the other character's response. The other character's slightest response will tell Leslie whether he is getting closer to the fulfillment of his want or whether he is beginning to lose what he has been wanting.

In summary, the actor is working at his best when he, as Leslie, has a vivid want at all times. Secondly, the actor's power is increased when his want is directed to a specific person, Georgia. And thirdly, the vitality of the want is amplified when Leslie's want is immediately dependent on a specific response from Georgia.

So we say that at the heart of every moment Leslie spends on stage there exists—

1. An ongoing want
2. A receiver
3. A desired response from the receiver

Before we go any further, it is essential to clear up a point about terminology. We have been discussing what we have called a system of wants. And we have defined this system as an interlocking series of verbs. Here is a list of terms. Each of these terms is used at various times by directors and teachers to describe the want of the character:

The OBJECTIVE
The GOAL
The PURPOSE
The AMBITION
The INTENTION
The DESIRE
The NEED
The PURSUIT
The ENDEAVOR
The VERB
What are you AFTER?
What are you trying to GET?
What are you DOING?
What are you PLAYING?

A great deal of confusion would be saved in our profession if all directors and teachers would use the same word to describe the want of the character. Most of the skilled directors I know use the word *objective* to describe Leslie's want. Communication in every rehearsal would be made more efficient if every actor could be brought to the realization that all the above words mean the same thing!

Each of the words in the list is intended to signify Leslie's want, and each of the words in the list requires a verb to illuminate his want. It is a pity that so many teachers have cluttered up the nomenclature. And it is consoling and liberating to the actor to discover that although he may work with ten different directors, each using a different name for the want of the character, all ten directors mean exactly the same thing. In deference to my teacher Allen Fletcher and to the tradition of Stanislavski, I encourage the use of the term *objective* to refer to the system of wants experienced by the character. The character moves from one objective to another through the course of the script. It is customary for each of the different objectives in a scene to be called *beats;* any given scene is composed of one beat after another. Each character maintains his own independent series of beats, and each beat changes at the moment when the objective, or want, of the character changes.

## THE QUEST FOR THE OBJECTIVE

The only real reason a director is needed in rehearsal is to perform the following function: persistently to draw the actor to a more meaningful and appropriate choice of objectives, and then to persuade the actor to lend his full commitment to those objectives. This is the purpose of a director. He helps the actor choose an objective and then encourages him to play it with all his heart. Any director who avoids this practice is wasting everyone's time. The entire goal of rehearsal, from beginning to end, is to draw the actor toward a strong, appropriate objective, and to persuade him to put his shoulder behind that objective and push hard. Relentlessly and continuously the director asks the actor, "What is your objective?" He consistently refuses to take an adjective or a noun for an answer. If the director does nothing more than continuously ask the actor for his objective, he will have a successful production. If he fails to ask the actor repeatedly what his objective is, there is the greatest likelihood that his production will fail.

Despite the fact that an actor is fervid, and despite the fact that acting is his life, most actors tend to resist acting. Although he deeply longs to be swimming in the water, the actor approaches the shore with great reluctance. A director is there to encourage him to go into the water. When an actor is acting well, he has taken on some degree of suffering. In lending his belief to the character, he consents to go through the passions of the character. Since no one really desires to suffer, there is a part of the actor that wants *not* to experience the deep and painful feelings of the character. Another part of the actor wants those experiences but would prefer to delay the real experience as long as possible. The actor tends to postpone making choices that would cause him pain. The actor does not want to pin himself down to experiencing the suffering of the character. He would rather indicate these passions for a while rather than go fully into them, because he knows that when he finally consents to go into them it will cause him some pain. He knows it is going to hurt him. To some extent it hurts to be "in" the character. "As long as I can stay outside the character, at least I am not suffering," he mutters subconsciously, "so I'll sketch in the feelings for a while in order to avoid going fully into a deep personal belief in those feelings."

Now, this is a resistance that is natural for almost all actors. The actor deeply wants to play the part, but he is reluctant to get into it. He would rather "indicate" the passions than feel them. The director's job—and here it is in a nutshell—is to persuade the actor away from giving the "representation" of the experience. The director persuades the actor to participate in the experience. To put it another way, the director coaxes the actor away from giving a demonstration of the passion and persuades the actor to go into the inner life of the character and actually experience the passion.

Every actor is slightly reluctant to make this transition. Some actors have never learned to make the transition. They are very poor actors. They spend their entire careers indicating the feelings rather than experiencing them. They are phony. They never actually experience the feelings of the character, whereas the entire art of acting is based on the performer's ability to sustain the experience of the inner life of the character.

So the director is there to persuade the actor away from the representation of the feeling and into the experience of the feeling itself. To do this the director uses one technique, and he uses it all the time. It saves a great deal of energy and confusion. Rather than lengthy discussions on the merits of each scene, and rather than delivering long directorial expostulations on the character, the skilled director simply asks one question relentlessly: "What is your objective?" At first the actor will not know. He will try to offer an adjective.

And so the question "What objective are you playing?" is repeated, and the director will only accept a verb as an answer. Pin the actor down; he probably doesn't want to be pinned down. There is safety in vagueness. There is comfort in "indicating." There is painlessness in remaining uncommitted. Actors tend to run like pigs in a barnyard to avoid pinning down the objectives. Frequently they will throw up a barrage of adjectives: "Well, you see his anger here, the pent up fury, the resentment from the past; he's really bitter, he's gotten cynical, he's sour; he's rejected, disillusioned, full of contempt, and it all erupts in a torrent of rage and recriminations and revenge . . ." And on and on he goes, flinging colorful adjectives and nouns about like confetti. This kind of waffling should be stopped. After the second sentence, the director should gently step in and say, "Those are adjectives. Please give me a verb." Once again the actor experiences a sense of resistance. He suddenly realizes that he is about to commit to experiencing the character's want and in the company of that want will come some discomfort, some suffering. "I think he probably wants to annihilate his wife." Immediately the actor has committed himself to experience a very painful desire. The director says, "Thank you for that verb; 'annihilate' is a very playable objective."

Gradually, the actor abandons this avoidance technique of hiding behind decorative emotional descriptions. Adjectives and nouns are of no use and must be avoided during the rehearsal. The skillful director limits what he says. He systematically draws the actors toward the right verb and encourages them to give their full personal commitment to that verb. This is the business of directing.

## INDICATING

Not all verbs are actable. But before proceeding to a discussion about refining the choice of verbs, let us once again give our attention to some terminology.

Here is a list of words that directors commonly use when they are criticizing an actor's work:

> you are GENERALIZING
> you are TELEGRAPHING
> you are INDICATING
> you are PLAYING ATTITUDE
> you are PLAYING the ADJECTIVE
> you are PLAYING RESULT
> you are MODE PLAYING
> you are BEING SCENIC
> you are DIRECTING YOURSELF
> you are ANTICIPATING
> you are ILLUSTRATING
> you are DEMONSTRATING
> you are MUGGING
> you are BEING PHONY
> you are UNBELIEVABLE

Each director has his favorite phrase, but all the above phrases mean exactly the same thing. Once again, we see how much simpler our profession would be if we were to establish a uniform vocabulary for our techniques. These phrases all carry the same message from the director to the actor. The message is this: "You are allowing yourself to represent a picture of the experience and avoiding a personal commitment to the want of the character." To put it another way: "You are indicating a feeling rather than playing your objective."

There is a value in the actor knowing which phrase a director customarily uses. But it is even more helpful for the actor to be aware that when he hears any of the phrases on the above list, they all mean, "You do not have an objective. Find one and play it."

## FINDING ACTABLE VERBS

Once we have persuaded the actor to respond with a verb when asked for his objective we have opened the door to creative acting. Now we have two refinements that will increase the effectiveness of these verbs. The first of these refinements might be called the preference for *actable verbs*. The second we shall refer to as *upgrading the verbs*.

Are all verbs equally actable? No. An actor will offer a wide variety of choices, but the director should be prepared to accept only the verbs that an ordinary person could get behind with his shoulder and push hard for at least ten minutes. This immediately eliminates the following classification of verbs.

**Intellectual verbs**    These usually come in packages of three syllables or more. They are lofty or elegant. No ordinary human being ever spent two seconds, much less ten minutes, pursuing them. *Cogitate,* for example, is the intellectual form for a more ordinary activity: *figure out.* No one can put his shoulder behind the frail verb *reciprocate,* but anyone could push hard on *get even.*

**Behavior or Condition verbs**    These verbs describe a state of being or an action that does not require a strong commitment of intent. They are usually reflexive or subconscious activities that can be accomplished without effort—*sleep, laugh, sneeze, cry, eat, wait,* or *stand* usually require no hard pushing.

**Existential verbs**    These verbs include those vast activities that go on without our volition. They are too vague to be endeavored in. For instance, one can hardly push hard for ten minutes on the verbs *to be, to exist, to die, to become, to live, to use, to try,* or *to think.*

**Adjectival verbs**    This classification is extremely subjective, and one director will consider a certain verb in this category to be dangerous, while another will consider it acceptable. The determining factor is this: Does the choice of the verb sound dangerously close to indicating—or playing the adjective? For instance we might discourage the use of a verb such as *argue,* because it slides so unnoticeably into the adjectival playing of *argumentative; charm* because it slides into being *charming; pity* leads to *pitiful; imagine* leads to *imaginative; deceive* leads to *deceptive,* and so forth.

**Trigger verbs**    These verbs depict actions that occur so quickly the doer could not pursue them for ten minutes: *shoot, slap, kick, kiss, touch, quit.*

**Actable verbs**    These verbs, it is worth repeating, are commonplace, gutsy activities that an ordinary person could put his shoulder behind and push hard for ten minutes. One can certainly work hard for a long time to *convince, excite, tease, encourage, destroy, prove, entice, intimidate.*

The following rough chart could be augmented and refined by any student of directing. It provides a graphic way of looking at actable verbs. Gradually the director becomes selective in listening to the actor; so that, for example, when the director asks, "What is your objective?" and the actor answers, "I want to castigate him," the director will suggest, "Give me the down-and-dirty form of 'castigate.' " The actor might say, "bawl him out"; "give him hell"; "curse him out." The director: "That's better, those are more actable. You can't put your shoulder behind 'castigate'; it disappears. But you can really push hard on 'give him hell!' Use the down-and-dirty form; it's more actable."

# VERBS

| ACTABLE | INTELLECTUAL | BEHAVIORAL or CONDITIONAL |
|---|---|---|
| *hurt* | reciprocate | walk |
| *inspire* | atone | sneeze |
| *suppress* | glean | cry |
| *incite* | repudiate | laugh |
| *enlighten* | reign | shout |
| *crush* | blame | run |
| *encourage* | mollify | eat |
| *lambast* | avenge | sleep |
| *explain* | vilify | sit |
| *organize* | obfuscate | stand |
| *destroy* | ruminate | fear |
| *prepare* | reinstate | like |
| *build* | postulate | endure |
| *ensnare* | avow | hiccough |
| *tease* | require | belch |
| *cheer up* | accomplish | wait |
| *reassure* | adjust | record |
| *justify* | narrate | see |
| *mock* | impugn | recover |

| EXISTENTIAL | ADJECTIVAL | TRIGGER |
|---|---|---|
| think | create | slap |
| use | aggravate | kill |
| try | discuss | shoot |
| be | argue | kick |
| live | forgive | touch |
| exist | charm | kiss |
| die | pity | quit |
| become | deceive | slice |
| create | pine | tweak |
| do | deplore | wince |
| need | adore | lock |
| intend | enchant | notice |
| hope | marvel | omit |
| love | loathe | meet |
| happen | grieve | flash |
| begin | judge | snap |

It becomes apparent that nearly seven-eighths of the verbs in spoken English are of absolutely no use to the actor. So we have, once again, narrowed the field of choices, enabling the director to focus his attention on a small list of very refined verbs that he will find himself using over and over again. It may seem astonishing to the novice, but frequently an experienced director comes to the sudden realization that play after play he is using the same small group of verbs. The actable verbs turn out to be a mere handful of words used over and over again, by character after character. The conditions that surround these actable verbs vary widely, and these different conditions give definition and color to the drama.

## UPGRADING THE CHOICE

In the early rehearsals, the actor is tentative and his choice of a verb may be weak, frail, thin. His choice may be a verb, but one that is not strong enough to throw one's shoulder behind. Particularly in the first scenes of a play, in which the playwright is wrestling with the artfulness of his exposition, the actor comes up with a shrug: "I'm merely *telling* him about the procedures around here." The director asks, "What would happen if we were to upgrade that objective?" For example, the actor gives us TELL, and the director suggests that it may be upgraded as follows:

> TELL
> INFORM
> RELAY
> DOCUMENT
> EXPLAIN
> PROVE
> CONVINCE
> OVERWHELM
> BOMBARD
> DEVASTATE
> ANNIHILATE
> OBLITERATE

Now, how would it be if, instead of *telling* or *informing* him of the procedures of the house, you were to *overwhelm* him with the procedures, or even *bombard* him with the procedures? The upgraded verb may seem outsized at first, but we remember that it is inevitably modified by the conditions or given circumstances of the scene and will therefore not appear to the audience as an exaggerated choice. The hefty size of an upgraded objective—its definiteness, its ability to be used like a club—will seem attractive to the actor. It gives him something tough and clear to grasp—something powerful, something to which he can easily lend full commitment.

Let us look at some other examples of the verb being upgraded.

| | |
|---|---|
| CHARM her | COMPLIMENT him |
| FASCINATE her | FLATTER him |
| DAZZLE her | PRAISE him |
| WIN her | REINFORCE him |
| MANIPULATE her | ENCOURAGE him |
| SEDUCE her | STRENGTHEN him |
| SURROUND her | FORTIFY him |
| OVERWHELM her | INVIGORATE him |
| DOMINATE her | ELEVATE him |
| VICTIMIZE her | EXALT him |
| CONQUER her | IMMORTALIZE him |
| TYRANNIZE her | LIONIZE him |
| POSSESS her | MONARCHIZE him |
| OCCUPY her | DEIFY him |

Some observations should be made at this point:

An actor may be "stuck" with a weak objective. When the director invites him to upgrade it, he does not force the situation. He suggests the possible options. He encourages the actor to broaden his thinking, to consider splashier possibilities, thus adding color and fervor to the beat.

The audience never sees the actor's choice. For example, suppose the actress is to say to her lover, "What a wonderful, kind, thoughtful person you are!" The audience will hear only those words. But the degree of her conviction will be revealed by the actress's secret choice: whether to *flatter* him, to *fortify* him, to *exalt* him, or to *immortalize* him.

Actors love poetic words and even words they may not understand. It could be quite meaningful to suggest to the actress who is praising her lover that she *oil* him, *smother* him, *consume* him, or *arouse* him. But the actress might respond to *lionize* him, because of its connotative rather than its exact explicit meaning. Even though she doesn't understand the meaning of the word, her imagination is captured by it, and she happily envisions her lover becoming a rampant lion as she speaks of him.

When we use this technique of upgrading the verb, we sometimes lose track, temporarily, of the second and third components of a well-constructed objective—that is, the receiver and the response. After the verb has been upgraded, we merely add them in; so that the progression goes this way:

<blockquote>

I want to FLATTER him.

becomes

I want to PRAISE him.

becomes

I want to STRENGTHEN him.

becomes

I want to GLORIFY him.

becomes, with the receiver and the response included,

I want to GLORIFY him into realizing his true worth.

</blockquote>

All this discussion of actable verbs and upgrading of choices pales by comparison when we come to consider two immensely powerful verbs—the giant crowbars of acting technique—*get and make.*

## THE CROWBARS: GET AND MAKE

No matter how much homework a director may do, it is impossible for him to know in advance all the objectives of all the characters in a play. If he did he would be straining badly and would also be obviating the purpose of rehearsal. But what if the director gets stuck? What if he doesn't have a clue to what the next scene is about? What if he is required to work rapidly with a script with which he is unfamiliar? What if he is tired, angry, or disinterested and can hardly bring himself to the quest, much less savor the subtle differences of choice?

Fortunately, we have a rescue tactic. It is an all-purpose, shortcut, surefire, knockdown, bring-'em-back-alive, fail-safe, self-cleaning, inexhaustible magic trick, which, no matter how crudely employed, will always work. It is the crowbar of directing and will always produce satisfactory results in bringing the actor close to the choice of the right objective. This powerful lever is the interchangeable use of the giant verbs *get and make*.

Either of the following questions will always get the director out of trouble:

"What are you trying to GET him to do?"

"What are you trying to MAKE him do?"

Some directors, desperate to cover for lack of preparation, manage to get through the entire rehearsal period on these two sentences alone. In fact there are some directors who, unable to be bothered with refinements, have built an entire career on these two handy sentences.

"What are you trying to GET from him?"

"What are you trying to MAKE him give you?"

These two questions require an answer from the actor, and the answer has built into it the three components needed for the most effective statement of an objective. The answer must—

1. Contain a verb: "I am trying to CONVINCE."
2. Contain a receiver: "I am trying to convince HIM."
3. Contain a desired response: "I am trying to convince him TO GO WITH ME."

"What are you trying to get him to do?" may be asked beat by beat, scene after scene. It will never wear out. It applies to the beginning, middle, and end of a play; to lead characters and extras; to verse and prose; to old and young; to rich and poor;

to active and passive; to real and imagined; to morning, noon, and night.

When there is any uncertainty about how things are going in any scene, the director merely inserts the crowbar:

"What are you trying to MAKE her do?"

"I'm trying to MAKE her relax, MAKE her cheer up, MAKE her smile at me."

Presto. Both actor and director have something to go on. The scene has been pried loose and is actable now. The objective may be changed, modified, refined, or upgraded later, but, at least for now, we have—

1. a verb
2. a receiver
3. a desired response

# The Rehearsal Process

## PREPRODUCTION HOMEWORK

Ideally the director could use eight weeks before rehearsal begins to prepare his script, but this is an ideal seldom realized. The director usually has to do his homework much more rapidly. From the time he agrees to direct a play until the first day of rehearsal, the director should read the script through many times and in many different moods. Sometimes he will read it rapidly and gather quick impressions; sometimes slowly and carefully, asking questions of the text, searching out details, and making notes.

During the repeated readings, the director begins to create a mental movie of how he sees the action unfolding. The key moments usually arise early. He trusts his intuition at every step. For those passages that may be unclear, he searches back and forth through the text for the answers.

The mental movie evolves of its own momentum. By reading the text frequently, the director discovers that a certain pattern of movement and a certain sound of voices will ride forward in his imagination. The most effective movement patterns for the actors will emerge in his consciousness in a seemingly inevitable way.

The concept of the mental movie is a powerful technique. If the director rereads the text often enough, it can't help but take form in his imagination.

In preparation, I frequently block the entire play using little soldiers, moving them around on a ground plan. I like to work on a half-inch scale because it helps me to visualize detail more easily. When I have swept through the play eight or ten times without stopping, I will begin slowly and methodically breaking the play into segments, which are commonly called beats. When I have determined all the beats in each act, I give my attention to each beat again and again, going over it to discover the objectives of the characters and to visualize their positions on the stage. The most intense visual or physical relationship of the actors usually occurs towards the end of each beat. It is impossible for the director to have worked out every single objective of each character. This would take too long, and it would tend to make the director too didactic in rehearsal.

Almost every play will have an intermission, but a director should never take for granted that the intermission is in the right place or that there are the right number of intermissions. In contemporary theatre two-act plays seem to be more popular than plays with three acts. Five-act plays are completely out of use. Some plays can be played in one long act without intermission. The placement of the intermission and the number of the intermissions is at the director's discretion. The deciding factor is usually the relationship between the weight of the material and the time it takes to unfold.

In planning the intermissions, the director always looks carefully at what we call the "curtain lines," the last line of text before the end of an act. As the mental movie is being formed, the director makes certain to find a key, dynamic way to close each act. In a similar way, the director gives attention to the entrances and the exits, but particularly to the exits of each character. It is important to squeeze the towel dry before the actor leaves the stage.

In the preproduction period, the director immerses himself in the world of the play. He tries to seek out the heart of the playwright. He tries to fold into his own body the animal vitality of the play. One great aid to absorbing the life of the script is for the director to read all the other plays by the playwright, together with his novels, essays, letters, and other writings. It is also very helpful to read reviews of previous productions of the play and to look at pictures of other productions. Reading the other works by the author aids the director in this very specific way: The director learns to appreciate the language of the author; he learns how the author expresses himself. He discovers what sorts of things are important to the author. He becomes aware of the author's use of leitmotif, symbolism, detail, humor, social attitudes, spiritual values. He also becomes aware of what messages the author considers important and what vision the author is striving to reveal. If the director can place the very heart of the playwright within his own breast, he will more successfully express the playwright's intent. Scenes from a playwright's novels will illuminate scenes in the play. When the director becomes completely absorbed in the style of the author, it is easy for him to know what is appropriate to the production. It is also easy for him to speak to the actors about the intent of the author. Having read all the author's work, the director is better able to evaluate where the author has actually succeeded in the script.

It is amazing how many plays have been printed and published that contain lines, passages, or whole scenes with which the author was dissatisfied—scenes he felt were incomplete or unnecessary. He may not have known how to fix them or how to bring them to life. Occasionally, a playwright will write a speech or a scene into a script because an actor or a director in the original production pressured him to do so.

The director's homework also includes making decisions that relate to the use of music and sound. He marks his script where he plans to introduce musical accompaniment or punctuation. He also indicates the places where sound effects will be needed.

When the director has completed his homework, he abandons it. When he approaches the first rehearsal, his mind is clear and he has created a strong mental movie. It is possible that he has worked out all the details of the actors' movements and written them in his script. The objectives, the blocking, and the mental movie may be completely realized in his mind. But as he enters the first rehearsal, he abandons all that work. The reason is this: He must not come into rehearsal with the entire production preconceived. He abandons his homework in order to allow the give-and-take of the rehearsal process to have its creative effect. Those ideas from his homework that are valid and compelling will come forward into his consciousness at the appropriate time; they will provide an effortless solution to problems; they will seem to answer the needs of the rehearsal at that moment. The only homework ideas he reveals to the actors in rehearsal are the ones that recur to him with a sense of compelling and inevitable rightness. The other ideas drop out of orbit and are replaced by the creative suggestions of the actors and other artists.

## DESIGN CONFERENCES

Each director relates to his stage designer and his costume designer in a unique and personal way. Many directors simply ask the designers: "How should it look?" The designers then go to their drafting boards and render the entire production in color.

Some directors enjoy working with a designer who designs both sets and costumes simultaneously. My experience has been that this overloads the designer. When one designer does both assignments, the following can occur: As one production was about to go into dress rehearsal I wanted to speak to the designer about something only to find that he was so harried, racing between the costume shop and the scene shop, that he felt my request to see him was an imposition. In cases in which one designer does both costumes and sets, he is usually so on edge, so nervous, and so overworked by the time of the dress rehearsal that a director may well feel guilty asking him to make any modifications in the production. In such cases, the designer heaves great sighs, falls asleep in the darkened aisles, and feels greatly imposed upon. This is not a creative situation. For this reason, I always request that a play have two designers, one exclusively for the sets and another exclusively for the costumes. By doing this, I have found that both designers are still healthy and approachable at the time of dress rehearsals.

In talking to the designers, it is important to begin discussion with a description of the general beauty. Leave discussion of mechanical details until a later time. In order to make the best use of the designer's creative imagination, it is valuable to begin by telling him what excites you about the play and why you find it beautiful.

In our early discussions, we agree on a metaphor. And both designers present ideas for the metaphors, such as photographs and paintings. It is essential that the director and both designers agree; there must be a three-way agreement on the methaphor, because the metaphor will be a limiting factor for all three of us in the preparation of the production. All three of us must feel enthusiastic and creative about the metaphor.

It is crucial that the director be specific in sharing his impressions. Be very open with the designers, tell them your secret thoughts about the play, tell them extraneous thoughts, thematic thoughts, impressions, dreams, resemblances, jokes. Tell them what the play reminds you of. Tell them in poetic terms, in dream terms, in casual terms, in peculiar terms. We take this impressionistic approach because the designers are listening for clues. We cannot be sure in advance what will awaken their imaginations, so we talk freely about our impressions. We talk generally and vividly about the peculiarities of the writing. We talk about the rhythm, the speed of the play, the movement, the color. We talk about every impression, and we ask the designers for their impressions of the play. And among this great salad of impressions, the director and the designers gradually find an image emerging that increases their mutual enthusiasm. The increased rightness of their ideas gives them a collaborative excitement. By the end of the discussion each designer's mind is bursting with impressions and feelings. It is important to let them go home with their thoughts, allowing time for gestation and synthesis. The designers will begin to see the *practique* emerging, and the design starts taking shape.

I always ask the designers to work in pencil and to come to

me with rough sketches, because once a designer has done a completed rendering, replete with detail and color, it is almost impossible to get him to change anything. It is better that his ideas be expressed in many sketches so that we can work together on changes and modifications. Together we reemphasize certain aspects, trim out the clumsy and the extraneous, and heighten the revelatory and the beautiful. After two or three reworkings of the rough sketches, I ask for ground plans and costume sketches in color, with sample fabrics.

Some directors are easy to please and use everything that is given to them by the designers. I tend to ask endless questions. "Will this coat have inside pockets? How many steps will it take to get upstairs? Will the risers be five inches, seven and one-half inches, or nine inches? Will the bannisters bear weight? Will the door slam? With a wooden sound or a metal click? Will the sofa be cushy? Will the panes of glass reflect light? Will the walls wobble? Does the actor have the right kind of legs for this costume? Will the hat shadow his eyes? Will the zipper show in the back? How many petticoats will this dress have? Linen, buckram, taffeta? How high are the women's heels? Are the soles of the shoes rubber? Which way do the shutters open? What can I see outside the window? How fast will the scene-change be? How is the hair to be dressed? Will there be enough room for the actor to sit on this corner? How long will the telephone cord be? Will the flowers look real?" I tend to plague the designer about these details, partly to assure myself, and partly to be prepared to tell the actor all about them. I want there to be as few surprises as possible when the technical rehearsal date arrives.

## TEXT PREPARATION

Should a director edit a script? Cut it? Rearrange the order of the scenes? Add lines? It seems to me that every script I have ever produced has had some changes in the text before it arrived on stage. There are some plays, like *The Cherry Orchard* or *Private Lives,* in which it is impossible to cut or alter one line. In these cases, one does them completely as written. There are other plays, such as the tragedies of Shakespeare, the Greek plays, the Restoration plays, which are simply too long for contemporary audiences if played uncut. The director should prepare his text *before* the first rehearsal. In plays that are too long, he must be very courageous and exact. One cuts the script to make it trim, stageworthy, and clear. If there are lines that are ambiguous, the director may add, change, or subtract words to bring out the maximum clarity. With great playwrights this is a delicate and responsible assignment, and one must have experience and a consummate skill with language before offering to rewrite even a word of Shakespeare or Sheridan. When working with a living playwright on a new play, one reads the text again and again with the playwright in order to be sure that the material is fully realized.

The most important consideration is this: All the changes that are to be made in the text should be made before the first day of rehearsal. One occasionally hears a director make a comment like this: "Well, we'll listen to it on the rehearsal floor and see how it sounds. If it seems too long, we'll cut it then." This technique is disastrous. In the first place, it doesn't work. And secondly, it causes the rehearsal to become a free-for-all among the actors and the director in which everyone has his say about what he thinks the best arrangement of the words may be. This destroys morale and it turns the playwriting function into a committee action.

Under no circumstances do I allow the actors to discuss whether certain lines or a certain scene should be cut or altered. I hope that during the time of my preparation of the text I have given sufficient attention to each individual line, so that I can defend that line to the actor and justify the need for that line in all its completeness. What about the text? Suppose, for example, the director takes a paperback edition of a play by Shakespeare and provides each of the actors with a similar copy of the play. They come to the first rehearsal; the director opens the paperback script and says, "We are about to do *Hamlet*. As written it would play five hours. Now take your pencils and I will read to you the cuts." This is the picture of an amateur director at work. I must confess that I have done this. But I have learned, to my great chagrin, that it is a very big mistake. The reason is this: If an actor even sees a line, he immediately considers it to be valuable. If you cut that line, he will resent it as though you had stolen something valuable from him. And if you cut his line in front of the other actors, he will tend to feel that you are picking on him and being more generous to the other players.

When the actors are all eager, fresh, and impressionable on the first day of rehearsal, it is very frustrating and discouraging to sit down and make laborious cuts in the text. The actors invariably find the experience a resentful one. It wastes time. It brings up questions in the actor's mind concerning the director's understanding of the play. It may invite the actors to doubt the director's discretion at the very outset, before the director has had an opportunity to enlist their support and enthusiasm. Under these circumstances, the actors frequently align themselves against the director from the very outset, deciding early on that he intends them no good, especially if he has cut so many of their treasured lines.

There is also the my-favorite-line syndrome. Working on the great classic plays, well-educated actors will frequently become very fond of certain lines or passages. Even in reading the uncut play through once, they may fall in love with certain lines. If the director starts the rehearsal by taking away what a leading actor may feel is his favorite speech or line, an animosity develops that may take weeks to dissolve.

The solution is this: In his homework the director cuts, edits, and arranges the text; he then takes it to a typist to have a clean, new script prepared. When he goes into rehearsal, the only lines that the actor sees are the lines in the typed script—the ones the director has chosen. If expense is a consideration, the director should buy twenty paperback editions of the text, gather his stage managers, and together they should pencil all the cuts into the texts. Then on the first day, the stage managers should distribute the amended scripts. A fully prepared script would be the least expensive and most valuable gift a director could give his actors. It's well worth the time and effort.

A strange fact is this: If an actor is presented with a completely cut script, with all the lines that are intended to be acted, for some reason it seldom occurs to him to go back to the original script and reread it to find those favorite lines. In these circumstances, the actors very seldom request to have a line put back in—if they do, their request should be taken seriously and dealt with in a special private session. I think my main interest in having the prepared text presented to the actors on the first day is this: The first day is a sensitive moment for the entire company. I want it to be a moment of enthusiasm and awakening. I want the song of the play to pour into their hearts. I want their imaginations to run playfully through the material, enlivening their excitement. This cannot happen if the parlance on the first day is filled with, "Now, page 14, three-quarters from the bottom, delete the words 'And just came through the window,' plus the following three speeches and over onto the top of the next page, concluding with the words 'That you could do such a thing.' " Instructions of this kind are invariably followed by comments from the actors such as, "Which page did you say it was? Can you repeat that line? Were those last three words included or not? You're not taking out the end of that speech, are you? Does that cut me out of that scene?" The complexity of such a discussion on the first day leads to a total drain on morale and must be avoided at all costs. We want the first reading to be pure, clean, simple, and joyful.

## THE FIRST READING

I have a few standard sentences that I say at the first reading of any play. No matter what the play is, my first readings are all alike. It is my intention as a director to make the first reading an eventless situation. I don't want anything interesting to happen at the first reading. I seat the actors in a circle, or around a table, and I always say these words before we begin: "Now, let us become acquainted with this play. We will read it *for sense only.*" I always stress that. "Please *don't act*. Please feel no obligation to give a performance of any kind." The reason I say this is that frequently an actor feels an obligation to prove to the other players that he is worthy of the role. He may feel compelled to show off his homework. Sometimes his enthusiasm is so great that he can't help creating special moments. All this must be inhibited, because if one actor starts to *act*, the others will feel compelled to act; pretty soon everyone will be so busy trying to act that no one will be listening to the play. Everyone will be competing to give some generalized kind of performance. It is impossible for an actor to give a good performance on the first reading—if he does, we are all in trouble.

I also say, "There will be words in the script that you don't know how to pronounce. When you come upon words that you don't know how to pronounce, just say 'jubajubajuba' and get through it somehow. Later we will clarify all pronunciation and sentence structure. If a sentence isn't absolutely clear to you in the first reading, it is all right. Get a general sense of it and go on. Simply find the sense of what you are saying and to whom you are speaking." Often an actor in the second or third week of rehearsal will suddenly discover that he has been saying a line to the wrong person. *"Oh, that's to you!"*

In the first reading there is no emotional expression except for those little hints of something to come that cannot be avoided.

## MEASURE OF SUCCESS

On the first day of rehearsal, I say very little about the play. At the beginning I may make a few general comments like, "We're very fortunate to have the opportunity to produce this masterwork. It's a very beautiful play." I may say a word or two about the general beauty, but I keep my comments to a minimum. I would rather have the actor become excited by the play than to have him overwhelmed with intellectual concepts or a description of my idea of the finished product. At the end of the reading on the first day, I usually say, "Thank you very much. Thank you for talking and listening to each other," or "Thank you for reading for sense." Any other comments are administrative. I ask the stage managers to make announcements about the schedule, the room, the lunch breaks, rehearsal skirts, footwear, and W-2 forms. The reason we turn to administrative announcements is that no time should be spent on esoteric or intellectual discussions. To this I make one exception. I call it "the measure of success."

I like to project for the actors some standard by which we all, the ensemble, may consider ourselves successful at the outcome. For example, "Let us consider the measure of our success on this production that we have a good time working together," or "Let us consider as the measure of our success for this production that we say yes to every creative idea and find out what happens," or "Let's consider as the measure of success for this production that we explore Chekhov's technique of indirect action to the fullest," or "Let's consider as the measure of success for this production that we drive our imaginations to new frontiers." Here is the reason: We take the pressure off the actor when we indicate that the measure of success is *not* popularity with critics or financial return at the box office. We want the actors to understand that the measure of success will *not* be rave critical notices, nor box-office success. Nor will the measure of success be a production that runs for three years and has five touring companies. In other words, it is important to describe the measure of success in such a way that the actor may make an evaluation of his work on the basis of the degree of his self-enhancement.

Where there is self-enhancement, there is happiness. True happiness is not giddiness or euphoria or ecstasy. The major characteristic of true happiness is that the self feels fulfilled, satisfied, enriched, witnessed, glorified. The self feels amplified. It feels consonant with nature; it feels a deep sense of personal achievement.

At the beginning of rehearsal, I try to direct the attention of the actors to a standard of self-enhancement. This relieves the actor of the responsibility to be funny or compelling to an audience. He knows that the director is with him in seeking a higher goal than merely having a hit. When one seeks a higher goal, excellence is always a result.

On the final day of rehearsal, I might then say, "At the beginning, five weeks ago, we said that the measure of our success would be that during the process of rehearsal we would all realize our better selves. Now let's evaluate the measure of success based on our original goal." Usually one can say, "We realized our goal and we have succeeded in that which we set out to accomplish. Now let's lean back against our achievement. Relax and enjoy playing the play!"

## SITTING REHEARSAL

For between three to five days after the first reading it is useful to keep the actors seated—around a table or using music stands to hold their scripts.

In the *sitting rehearsal* the most important thing is contact between the actors. Before getting on their feet the actors need an opportunity to explore their scripts. Try to get them to lean across their scripts to establish eye contact with the person with whom they are talking; and strive to evoke their objectives, no matter how vaguely formed they may be at the time. In the early stages we seek to establish eye contact and moment-to-moment truthful talking. Also, during the sitting rehearsal, we learn to pronounce all the names correctly and we resolve uncertainties about offstage life; that is to say, we make sure that each actor knows when he is to enter; where he is coming from; and where he is going when he leaves the stage. Cover this information at the table in advance. The actor will save you a lot of time later on by coming in through the right door without being told.

There's something else that has to be established in the sitting rehearsal. This is a very peculiar occurrence, but it happens all the time: Actors frequently will not know that they are supposed to be in a certain scene. Sometimes they don't even discover it until the blocking rehearsals, at which time an actor may suddenly bolt from the sidelines and say, "Oh, I'm in that scene! I didn't realize I was supposed to be there. I don't have any lines." Make sure that everyone who is in a certain scene knows that he is in that scene during the sitting rehearsal. It saves a lot of confusion when it comes time to block.

Some directors like to put a play on its feet immediately. I prefer to spend at least three or four days reading for sense, asking questions about the offstage life of the character—why a character does a certain thing or how his objectives fall into groups. In the sitting rehearsal, I establish the age of each character and his past relationships. The actor is encouraged to start thinking in the form of biography. You sketch in the objectives by asking him very broad questions like, "What do you think he's after in that scene?" "What is his objective in that scene?" or "What is he going for?" There is great value in keeping your words in the form of questions during the early rehearsals. You have to allow the play and the actor to speak to you. Invite the actors to fill in the answers to the questions you pose. As they fill in the answers, their ideas will enrich and enhance the ideas that have come from your homework; and thus you will be able to work together in a new, creative, and mutually responsive way.

## BLOCKING

When we talk about *blocking* we mean the patterns of movement of the actors on the stage. The blocking is evolved in a collaborative way between the actor, who has to do the moving, and the director, who can see what looks best and what is most appropriate to the action. After the sitting rehearsals, when the director is satisfied that the cast has a clear understanding of the script, it is time to begin putting the play on its feet.

The director describes the ground plan in great detail, so that the actors can visualize the set. If possible, he gives them a picture or a model of the set, which is provided by the designer. It is important for the actors to visualize the locale. With the ground plan marked in tape on the floor, the director walks the entire set, showing the cast each of the doors and windows, describing which way they open. He tries to have facsimile pieces of furniture placed in the room so that the actor can become familiar with the surroundings. The director takes the initiative by suggesting to the actor that he come through this door, or that he move to the sofa, or that he go up the stairs. It's best not to let the actors wander around the set with their scripts. Some directors say, "Well, let them get on their feet and go wherever they feel like going for the time being." An actor doesn't appreciate that. He likes to be given a framework, and then he can request changes in the framework; if the blocking he is given feels comfortable, it immediately increases his understanding of the play. Good blocking will always make the actor feel eager and enthusiastic, because he feels that the moves give him an opportunity to reinforce the feelings of the character.

Bad blocking will always make the actor feel uncomfortable. There are two goals in blocking: the first is to convey to the audience the maximum story-telling value, by having the actors take positions that reveal their emotional condition. The second goal of good blocking is that the actor should not only feel comfortable, but that he should feel *fortunate* to be able to move where you have asked him to go—that he senses his position on the stage helps to reinforce what he is trying to convey.

## WHEN DO YOU BEGIN TO BLOCK?

Successful directors have various blocking techniques. Some fine directors put the play on its feet on the first day of rehearsal. Some keep the actors seated until they become frustrated sitting down and start bolting from their chairs as they read. A director may vary his technique on the basis of the style of the play he is doing. Frequently a director will keep a Chekhov play in the seated phase for eight to twelve days before allowing the actors to begin walking. Whereas the same director approaching a Feydeau farce may put the actors on their feet the first day. As a general rule, it is advisable to keep the actors seated until they know what they are saying and to whom they are speaking—until they pronounce all the words correctly; scan the verse, where applicable, in correct cadence; and establish eye contact with their fellow players. In an average production, the period of seated readings is complete after four or five days. Then blocking begins.

## DO YOU DICTATE THE MOVES OF THE ACTORS?

It is a very poor idea for the director to read his blocking to the actor out of a prompt book. The director must have his blocking memorized. The rehearsal becomes a shambles if he runs back and forth to the book crying, "I think you cross left on, let me see, what was that line?" What is even more pitiful is to see a director standing at the center of the stage reading moves out of his text, losing his place, and demonstrating his lack of familiarity with the content of the scene. He must have the blocking memorized.

Every director in the profession has found himself on some occasion completely unprepared to block the scene. On these occasions it it best, first, to let the script block itself. "Where does it say you should enter from?" "Where have you just been?"

## WHAT HAPPENS WHEN THE ACTOR DISAGREES WITH YOUR BLOCKING?

There are two approaches to this situation. The first, which usually works with facility, is to say candidly to the actor: "What we are doing at the moment is a rough draft of the moves. It is not final. We will probably change it many times before we arrive at the best solution. But I ask you to go with me, merely for the time being, until we have sketched in the scene. Later, if you still feel awkward, we will certainly change it. I want you to be comfortable." If there is a liberal feeling of give-and-take within the company, this approach usually works.

On the other hand, a given actor may, for reasons of insecurity—as with stars or older actors—present a negative front. Frequently, he is testing the director or competing for attention. When an actor resists the initial blocking with comments such as, "Oh, my character wouldn't do that!" or "I can't motivate that," or "That doesn't work for me," the director must exercise patience and tact.

Perhaps he persuades: "Do it as a favor for me now and if need be we'll fix it later." If the actor is rigid, another approach might be temporarily helpful: "Where would you like to go? Where do you want to be? Let's try that for the time being and see how it works."

By presenting a positive spirit of collaboration, the director may win the actor over. But something more creative may occur. By using the actor's idea the director may be required to rethink values he had overlooked, and the actor's suggestion may lead to a completely new and more creative flow for the scene.

If an actor resists *all* the blocking, he should (1) be taken aside and his cooperation enlisted, or (2) be abandoned by the director, and left to wander about for a few days while the director blocks the other players—in such cases the actor usually is eager to be given specific blocking after a day or two.

## DO YOU REQUIRE THE BLOCKING TO BE WRITTEN?

We ask that the actor carry a pencil with his script for every blocking rehearsal—whether he boasts a good memory or not. We ask him to write the blocking down as it is given; when the blocking is changed, we take the time for the actors to erase the old blocking and to write the new blocking in the script. This may seem a mere formality, but there is nothing worse than to have the entire cast, two or three days after the blocking has been given, turning to the stage manager and asking, "Where did I go here?" "Am I supposed to be on the left or the right?" "Did I come down here?" "Was I supposed to cross there?" The confusion demoralizes everyone. I always make certain that each actor brings a pencil with an eraser to the blocking rehearsals.

A second, and possibly more beneficial, reason for having the actors write the moves precisely in their scripts is this: When an actor is working alone at home, the memory of the movements will play a profoundly important part in the actor's ability to memorize his words. The more specific the moves the easier it is to memorize.

## WHEN SHOULD THE BLOCKING BE COMPLETED?

It seems that no two productions have the same period of time for rehearsal. Whether the play is rehearsed in one week, as in summer stock; in four to five weeks, as with a repertory or Broadway production; or over eight to ten weeks of part-time rehearsals, as occurs in community or college productions, there is always one point at which blocking should be complete. The director should devise his rehearsal plan so that the cast is allowed at least three or four full runthroughs of the play before the elements of sets and costumes are added.

When the actor confronts his costume, wig, makeup, sets, and lights, he undergoes a tremendous change in focus. It is absolutely essential that he run through the play several times before that shift in focus occurs. The reason is this: In the rehearsal studio the actor's chief goal is the realization of the inner life of the character. He uses the runthroughs to make that inner life concrete; to give it continuity and flow; to experience the through-line of the story; and to test the boundaries of the entire structure of his performance. Only then is he able to enter the technical phase with confidence.

Woe to the director who, by mismanaging his time, is forced to take his production into technical rehearsals without having blocked the last half of the third act. The major source of trouble in such a case is that the actor falls into a state of panic. He has not run through. He is not complete. He has never experienced the confidence of "having a show." His panic infuses the production with an epidemic of desperation. All eyes begin to glaze. Small difficulties become monumental obstacles. Gossip, resentment, insecurity, and retaliation run rampant through the cast. The entire company anticipates disaster. They grasp at absurd and neurotic self-rescue techniques. They isolate themselves from one another and from the director. More often than not, their frustration spills over into open and aggressive confrontation with the director, the costumer, or anyone nearby.

In short, one of the most devastating mistakes a director can make is to miscalculate his rehearsal hours. One must never spend so much time on the "front end" of the play that the "back end" goes unblocked and unrehearsed. Even in a four-day rehearsal period, no matter how sketchy the blocking or how sloppy the early and middle scenes, *always* save enough time to block and run the final scenes. Miscalculation on this point inevitably creates one of those catastrophes that a young director only has to experience once in order to learn the consequences.

## COMPOSITION AND PICTURIZATION

To be precise, *composition* and *picturization* are both aspects of blocking. We deal with them separately because each contributes to the success of the blocking in different and specific ways.

Composition is the aspect of blocking that is mechanical.

> Downstage-center is the strongest position on the stage.
> Upstage-left is the weakest position.
> Facing full front is strong, full back is weak.
> Elevated positions take focus.
> Crosses from up-center to down-center are powerful.
> Crosses from stage right to stage left follow the "reading" line in Western culture.
> An individual standing separated from a group has focus.
> Symmetry connotes formality or ritual.

And on and on; there are many axioms about position that a director should know in order to create the most powerful stage composition.

Picturization is an aspect of blocking that intensifies the story-telling values.

A dead body tends to be horizontal.

A person kneeling before a person standing is connotative of begging.

A column of men standing at attention has a military connotation.

A boy and girl holding hands connote lovers.

A man pointing a pistol connotes a threat.

A man carrying the limp body of a baby connotes a parent bearing a dead child.

Every position of the human body carries with it a connotation for its mental and emotional condition. Picturization is a reinforcement, by position, of all relationships, so that even a deaf person could follow the action clearly by watching the movements, the positions, and the gestures.

Picturization is similar to choreography in that the body positions reveal the relationships, independent of the words. My productions usually bear a slight resemblance to ballets, because I tend to picturize as intensely as possible. For example, in my production, when the script calls for two people seated on opposite sides of a table, the one who is winning is usually climbing over the table, and the one who is losing is sliding under the other side.

Picturization is the technique of placing the actor in the positions that reveal and reinforce the story or the psychological disposition of the character. Picturization is absolutely necessary in every successful production. It is a technique that, if used correctly, will always increase the success.

When I started directing, I didn't know where to place the actors. All my thoughts were arbitrary. I saw no reason why the characters couldn't just stand around talking to one another. One might just as easily sit on the sofa, the chair, the stool, the window seat, the railing, or the bottom step. It seemed to me that there were a thousand choices. There is, however, only one optimum choice—only one really good, revealing choice. If the director hunts for the most revealing picturization of each moment, the play will be very clear to the audience, because the movements will tell the story without the dialogue. Secondly, the actor will feel comfortable and confident because he senses he is in the positions that are most revealing. Thirdly, the accumulated picturizations tend to intensify the drama because each moment is maximized. In other words, the most revealing position for the dramatic material is being demonstrated on a moment-to-moment basis throughout the entire production. A fourth benefit, somewhat more remote but just as practical, is that if the production is well picturized, it will be easy at a later time to put in an understudy or replacement for a given part. All the actor has to be given are the movements of the character, and he will immediately understand what the scene is about, what the intent of the director is, and what the objective of the character is; he will feel comfortable, relieved, and secure. When you evolve the clearest picturization for a character, any actor, even a poor actor, can play the part and "look good."

Picturization is not a personalized technique. It does not vary from one director to another or from one play to another. It is a system of connotative body language that is innate in all human culture. This connotative body language transcends spoken language. The system is equally revealing in Russia and Africa. Its message is the same in Spain, in Egypt, in China, and in New York. Its language has remained unchanged since Hellenic Greece. Every skilled director knowledgeably or intuitively uses this technique of connotative body language.

For a more specific understanding of the techniques of composition and picturization I refer the reader to the definitive work on these two subjects: *Fundamentals of Play Directing* by Alexander Dean and Lawrence Carra, chapters 7 and 8. These two chapters changed my directorial career. I regard them as absolutely essential; I credit the majority of my directorial success to a perpetual and inviolate reliance on chapters 7 and 8. In my opinion a director's professional success is based on his understanding of the principles revealed in these two chapters.

## MEMORIZATION

During the rehearsal period, an inexperienced director is unprepared to encounter two standard moments of severe depression. It is good to anticipate these moments and to understand that nothing can be done about them. One must devise techniques merely to get through them.

The first moment occurs in the rehearsal at which the actors are supposed to be off book for the first time. The first off-book rehearsal is always a disaster. The young director should understand that when the actors go off book for the first time, all the work achieved in rehearsal to that date—blocking, nuance, relationship, understanding of the situation, even contact and truthful talking—goes out the window. The director has to understand that it's not his fault the rehearsal has fallen apart. One must expect it. Anticipate it. Only after he has directed fifteen or twenty plays is a director seasoned enough to shrug his shoulders and say, "Oh, they went off book today, so, of course, everything was a muddle." The moment they go off book, the actors turn into hopeless clods bumping into furniture and saying, "Can you give me that line again? I thought it was the other way around. I had it perfect in the bathtub this morning. No, don't help me. What is it? I thought I knew it."

An experienced director knows there's nothing he can do at this phase of rehearsal. Young directors usually don't expect this letdown to occur, this blues period, and frequently they feel depressed when it happens. They go home in despair saying, "Nothing happened in rehearsal today. We didn't make any progress." When the actors are getting off book, there seems to be no progress. The progress is getting off book. The director has no choice but to doodle on his clipboard. He cannot take notes; he cannot make suggestions; and at this time he should avoid asking questions such as, "What is your objective?" Just watch the actors. While they are wrestling with their lines, the director must sit in patience. At the end of the rehearsal he says, "It's getting better. Be sure you know your lines perfectly by tomorrow." Then he goes home.

## WHEN DO YOU TELL THEM TO BE OFF BOOK?

I never tell them suddenly, "Let's do this without books tomorrow." I give them plenty of notice. On Monday I announce, "By Thursday, you should know the lines for this scene." We work the scene Tuesday; and on Tuesday I say, "Try to get the lines out by Thursday." On Wednesday, I say once again, "In this scene you probably ought to be word perfect by tomorrow." Then on Thursday I say, "Okay, now let's try it without books."

You have to prepare them. Tell them in advance when they have to be off book; but most actors will have to be pushed a little to get off book. If they carry the book too long, the phase of rehearsal in which the scene should come to life will go past and they will still be hampered by the book. They will miss "the coming to life" of the scene because they don't know the words. It's your job to require the actor to be off book in time for the scene to come to life.

## DO YOU EVER ASK THAT ALL LINES BE MEMORIZED BEFORE THE FIRST REHEARSAL?

Some directors ask the actors to have all their lines learned by the first rehearsal. They don't know what it's like to be an actor. An actor doesn't believe that learning all his lines before the first rehearsal is a creative thing to do. If however there is a very short rehearsal period, or if the play is a movement comedy and the words are not difficult to learn, it may be worth thrusting your company into panic for the first few days. Unfortunately, in this situation, the actors memorize many mistakes. They mispronounce words; they have the grammar incorrect; their sentences don't make sense; and three or four weeks later, you find yourself still correcting them for mistakes they have memorized incorrectly. One puts a pebble in an actor's shoe by asking him to memorize before he understands.

The ideal is for the memorization to be effortless or almost unnoticeable. You should run through the material so many times that the words all seem necessary to the achievement of the objective. The books just slide out of their hands; they may need one or two little coachings here and there, but the reason they know their lines is that they have done them so many times that all the words have become necessary and useful.

## WHAT ABOUT ACTORS MEMORIZING THE LONG ROLES?

When an actor has a long part it's sometimes good to assign an assistant stage manager to go over lines with him. By working this way the actor is not required to ask his wife or lover to hear his lines—if he has a lengthy role, his wife or lover doesn't want to hear all those lines over and over again anyway. There's a great advantage in assigning someone to the actor simply to routine the words.

In plays in which there are only two roles, each of the actors has approximately fifty percent of the lines to memorize; which means that in a two-act play each actor has the equivalent of an entire act to memorize. When working with only two actors, it's unprofitable to work for more than five hours in a single day. If you try to work for seven hours, you will notice the diminishing return after five hours to be dramatic and frightening. You see the actors' eyes start to cross; they begin to disagree unreasonably; they fret about illusions; they get confused; they forget things; they drop things; they bump into things; they say, "I'm so sorry, will you give me that line again? Where are we?" In other words, their minds simply refuse to function. In a two-character play, never rehearse longer than five hours at a time.

## THE WORKING REHEARSAL

After the actors have memorized the text, one can really go to work testing and retesting the objectives. We call these the working rehearsals. In each case, I call each scene individually and work on it in three phases, as discussed in relation to the learning process. One tries one's own ideas; one tries the actor's ideas; and together, suitable and appropriate decisions are made. At the end of each rehearsal, we take a short "walkthrough" of the scene to demonstrate the changes and adjustments introduced that day. A walkthrough is a less intense reenactment of the new blocking. The working rehearsals are usually fun. They should certainly be playful. They are the most creative time for both the actors and the director, the time of adventure. The actors are free of the text, so they are able to be flexible. They have also studied their objectives sufficiently so that they welcome suggestions to upgrade them, vary them, modulate them. With the working rehearsal a sense of throughline begins to come into the scene. Occasionally, a passage will even leap to life, encouraging everyone in the room, giving them the sense that we are on the right track.

## IMPROVISATION

Specific kinds of improvisation during the rehearsal period can be useful. Improvising, however, can also be a very dangerous technique. A director must be very skilled in the use of this technique for it to work in a creative way. He must know—

1. Which plays are suited to the use of improvisation
2. At what time during the rehearsal period improvisation can be utilized
3. Which material should be improvised
4. How the improvisation should be structured so that the actors will derive the maximum benefit from it

Before going into more detail, I should make it clear that there are two distinct types of improvisation. There is one type of improvisation that is designed to awaken the offstage life of the characters in the play, and to awaken the actor's sense of the historical period, the nationality, the customs and mores of the world of the play. This type of improvisation also aids the actor in discovering the movement, voice, and timing patterns of the character, as well as his attitudes towards the other characters.

The second type of improvisation, one which a knowledgeable director very seldom uses, is aimed at a special problem. It occasionally happens that an actor is unable to reach some key emotional material, either because the material is too sensitive to him and he wishes to avoid it, or because the material is so remote that he is unable to find a parallel in his memory of personal experience. A director may suggest the use of improvisation in order to draw the actor closer to the material. A carefully selected and supervised improvisation can be helpful in a stubborn case in bringing strong emotional response to the foreground. This second type of improvisation is seldom used, because, for one thing, if the actor is a professional actor, he is usually proud of his ability to express any emotion that is requested of him. In a certain context, it is an insult to ask an actor to improvise on emotional material. Secondly, directors who use this technique are frequently pretending to play psychiatrist. These directors like to get their psychological tweezers into an actor's personal makeup and start playing games with his extremely sensitive inner life. This is very dangerous. These directors usually don't know what they are doing, and, in most cases, do nothing to aid the production. I don't rule out this particular technique completely. I've used it about three times to great effect and I have known very talented directors to use it occasionally with good results. But a director who improvises strong and deeply rooted emotional material on a habitual basis is suspect. Most actors find working in this way very upsetting. Usually the rehearsal period doesn't allow enough time to put the exploded pieces back together.

Let us give our attention to the first purpose of improvisation, that is, the offstage life of the characters.

**In Which Plays Is This Technique Useful?**     It is most profitable in naturalistic or realistic plays. For example, to improvise the offstage life of characters from Chekhov, Ibsen, Williams, Miller, O'Neill, Inge, or Wilson could be extremely valuable, awakening the imagination of the actor and filling in many colors. Plays that lend themselves very poorly to improvisation are the works of Shaw, Sheridan, Congreve, Shake-speare, Sophocles, T. S. Eliot, Dylan Thomas, Christopher Fry, Tom Stoppard. What immediately appears to be the strongest characteristic of these authors is their heavy and extremely individual use of language. If one were to improvise these authors, it would impose considerable discomfort on the actor. The actor asks, "Am I required to improvise in the manner of speech used by the playwright?" Very few people can improvise in iambic pentameter. So that improvising Shakespeare is very difficult, if not virtually impossible, and is usually laughable. Even if one left the iambic pentameter aside it would be very difficult to improvise using "thee" and "thou," "comest," "goest," "hither," "thither," "my liege," and so forth as one's natural parlance. Shaw is also difficult to improvise for the reason that his characters are usually so busy promoting ideas that actors simply find it impossible to invent words rapidly enough to keep up with the characters' thinking. It may be possible for actors to improvise comfortably in the language of an author whose writing is highly stylized, but it has never worked successfully for me. Let's give our attention to Chekhov, because it is when working on his plays, and on plays by authors like him, that improvisation is most useful.

**At What Time in Rehearsal Do We Introduce Improvisations?** After the first week or ten days it may be a good idea to hold one improvisation; another two or three days later; and then another perhaps after a week. The improvisations should act as companion pieces to the working rehearsals. I would never interrupt the rehearsal period for three or four days of exclusive improvisation. Improvisations should be regarded as gifts to the actors, which they receive as corollary illuminations to the regular process of rehearsal. During any normal rehearsal period, one is likely to have time for approximately three to seven complete improvisations. It's good to limit an improvisation to between forty-five minutes and an hour.

**What Do We Improvise?**     To begin with, we do not improvise material that has already been written by the author. That is to say, we do not paraphrase the text—paraphrasing is a different and often helpful technique; it is especially helpful during the rehearsals of language plays by playwrights such as Shakespeare or Shaw.

What we do select to improvise is what we call the offstage life. For instance, in act 2 of Chekhov's *Ivanov*, Dr. Lvov and his tubercular patient, Anna Petrovna, make an entrance into their neighbor Lebedev's drawing room. Perhaps we would improvise the two of them riding through the snowy night on their way to Lebedev's estate. As they ride in the sleigh, the actors' conversation, and their imagined sensory experiences of the chilling wind, of the muffled sound of the horses' hooves on the snow, or of the rumble of the timber on the bridge awaken thoughts that will be helpful when the couple join the party guests.

Another example of a useful improvisation would be a picnic at which all the major characters of a play meet by the river under the shade of an immense tree. One sits whisking at flies with a handkerchief. Another drinks too much vodka. A young lady reads from a book of poetry, and a student philosophizes. A young girl makes a wreath of summer flowers for her boyfriend. An old lady sits by the samovar and slices cucumbers. A doctor peers out over the horizon trying to postpone his departure. This kind of improvisation helps the actor to awaken his offstage life and his relationships with the other characters. The major characteristic of this kind of improvisation is that it is innocent; it does not contain heavy dramatic material. It contains easily manageable material, easy conversation, easy activity. No emotional showdowns are called for. The purpose of the improvisation is to awaken the actor's imagination to the total life, the total experience, of the character. The intent is to awaken the inner life of the character for short passages of time; after one has done three or four improvisations, the actors find that their sense of inner life begins to develop longer and longer passages of continuity. When this happens, they find that they can carry their inner life from the improvisation over into the dialogue of the script.

**How Should the Improvisation Be Structured?** The director should tell the actors in advance how long the improvisation will last. He should tell them that he will stop them when it is over. He should set up a very specific place—at the beach, on a bus, at a Sunday afternoon dinner, at a picnic. He should set up the physical circumstances as completely as possible, involving as much furniture as may be necessary to describe completely the physical surroundings. I find it of great value to add food to the first two improvisations. Food gives the actors something to do. When an actor discovers how his character eats, it is usually a revelation, and it unlocks many other doors. It is desirable for the director to give each actor one strong, unifying objective for the improvisation. One mustn't turn them loose and say, "Find something to do." It's better to begin by making suggestions such as, "Try to interest your niece in the pamphlets that have just arrived from Moscow," or "Get the student to tell what he would do if he controlled the government," or "Get the soldier to tell you the details of his last campaign," or "Persuade your uncle not to drink so much," or "Get the doctor to change his plans about leaving." Use simple objectives. As the actor begins improvising he may drop the objective you have suggested in favor of another that commands his attention. It will invariably be much more imaginative and revealing. But, giving him a simple objective at the beginning of an improvisation is a necessary springboard.

I watch the improvisation very carefully, and if I see it going off the track, I will occasionally approach one of the actors and whisper a new objective that may throw the scene in a new direction. Sometimes I will have one or two actors sitting with me at the side who have not yet entered the improvisation. When I see how the improvisation is developing, I might mutter an objective to them and send them into the improvisation with a new stimulus or a new piece of information that will cause the improvisation to go in a new direction. I am on guard for any sign of emotional distress, because while some emotional experience is desirable, one must be ready to jump in and halt the improvisation if an actor begins to develop material of an hysterical nature, or material that contains an exaggerated emotional experience. It happens only occasionally, but one must watch for the possibility. The early improvisations should be structured more like exchanges of information between the characters; whereas the later improvisations can contain stronger experiential exploration. By information exchanges I mean this: The first improvisation does not seem like an improvisation at all. The director instructs the actors to ask each other questions about themselves. "Please answer each other in the first person." So the questioning may go something like this: "You arrived in our town when you were twenty-two. Where were you before that?" "Where did you live in Paris?" "What was your house like?" "Do you have any political views?" "What type of school did you go to?" "I understand that you were married before and that your wife is deceased." "What was she like?" "Did you have any children?" "How did she die?" The actors ask questions of each other that will lead to information about their pasts in the first person singular. This is a very valuable way to design the first improvisation. The actors find it enjoyable, because they are freed from the obligation to invent plot, conflict, or dynamically interesting scenes.

The second improvisation will have a bit more form; for instance, a picnic or a Sunday dinner. The third improvisation may be a carriage ride, or a gathering in an anteroom at the opera, or at a private supper after the threatre. The fifth and sixth improvisations may involve more intimate, dramatic material. For example, when working on Chekhov's *Uncle Vanya* it is valuable to improvise the three or four minutes that occur offstage when Vanya runs to find the pistol with which he intends to shoot the professor. This scene would reveal what Yelena and the others say to Vanya offstage as they try to persuade him to calm down. When correctly structured this improvisation could be used by the actors in the offstage area during the actual performance of the play.

## RUNTHROUGHS

After the play has been blocked and the actors have worked through each act, it is a good idea to walk through each act without stopping before going on to the next act. The walk-through should be slow and methodical. Tell the actors that you do not expect performances. "Let us try to get a through-line for the act—to see what we have, to find out where the rough spots are." It is helpful if all lines have been learned and books are gone before the walkthrough.

When each act has had a walkthrough, it is time to put them all together. Give the company three or four days' notice of your plan to run through so that they may prepare mentally for it. They will scurry about finding facsimile props; locating comfortable boots, rehearsal skirts, spectacles; writing out prop letters; learning last-minute lines; and organizing their sequence of entrances. Finally, they are ready for a runthrough of the entire play.

Some directors who have never acted make a terrible mistake: They call for a runthrough in the second week of rehearsal. They jump from the initial blocking rehearsals directly to runthroughs, omitting the very valuable phase of working each scene until the actor is comfortable. Some directors I have known spend the entire rehearsal period running through. They run through in the morning, break for lunch, and run through again in the afternoon. Any actor who has experienced this kind of rehearsal period will quickly tell you, "It is insanity." The actors must spend the vast middle period of rehearsal working and reworking the scenes. Then about five days before the first technical the actor is hungry for a runthrough to put all the pieces together.

It is very important for the director not to interrupt the runthrough under any circumstances. Before a runthrough, I usually say to the actors, "You may run into difficulty here or there, but no matter what happens, keep the action going. I understand that there will be props missing; I understand that you may not remember all your lines; I understand that there are some new sound cues that you are getting used to, and that the cues may not work. But do your best to keep going through the play without stopping. If something goes wrong, try to absorb it or get past it in any way you can. Try not to stop under any circumstances."

This approach usually pressurizes the actor into continuity. Many uncertainties will resolve themselves; many questions will answer themselves; various meanings will break into the clear for the first time, and sections of the inner life will suddenly lock into place. Transitions will become automatic and the actor will begin to experience the through-line of the role. The story will become more alive for him. If one actor stops, then another actor will stop, and a third actor will stop, and thus ensues the breakage of the very thing we are trying to achieve.

When something goes wrong, the actor, feeling compelled to continue, will receive an adrenalin rush that will help him to get past the difficult moment, and frequently that adrenalin rush will carry with it a creative explosion—a creative solution to a problem that helps to enliven the scene and give coherence to the through-line. The necessity to keep going becomes the mother of invention.

It is wise to plan at least four or five runthroughs in the studio before going onto the stage for the first technical rehearsal. The reason for the runthrough is essentially to force continuity into the work. During the runthrough the director must keep his mouth shut. He will write many notes to give to the actors afterwards.

Some directors arrive at their technical rehearsal without ever having run through the play from beginning to end without stopping. This is very sad. It is destructive to the actor's confidence. It indicates that the director lacks control of his use of time.

As soon as the production goes onto the stage everything will seem to fall apart. The actor's attention will be on the physical aspects of the stage—the lights, the furniture, the costumes, and so forth. In order to survive the technical rehearsals without panic, the actor needs a confident memory—an image of the entire story at a full-throttle experience level. He has to have had the full emotional experience of the play before he approaches the technical rehearsal.

## NOTES

When you give notes, always try to go as fast as you can in order to keep the complete attention of the entire cast. Sometimes there is a tendency for a director to start to give a note to one actor and to become so involved, to go on at such length, that all the other actors get bored, start talking among themselves, and lose track. If you keep the notes very short and keep the entire attention of all the actors, each of the actors will be listening and they'll know what you're talking about when you suddenly turn to them and say, "This affects you too." "You should be prepared when she does this," or something of that nature. Another thing to do with notes is to add the words: "Do you understand?" or "Do you see what I mean?" or "Do you get it?" or "Is that okay?" Add that little phrase at the end of each note; it helps you to keep the note short. Sometimes, an actor knows exactly what you're talking about and you don't have to take twelve paragraphs to describe it. But, sometimes, you take a chance and you give the actor a short note. When you've given him the short note and said, "Do you understand?" and he says, "Yes," you're in. If you've given him a short note and he says, "No, I don't," then you can take your time to elaborate. If they don't understand it after that, tell them to stay after and you'll show them. That helps you to keep the note session moving. You have to go very rapidly. It will become debilitating to the actors if the director uses the opportunity merely to talk.

## THE FITTING ROOM

When it's time for the actor to put on his costume and wig for the first time, he invariably feels betrayed. He is usually horrified at the distance between the way he looks and the way he had imagined he was going to look in the role. This is customary. Very seldom will the actor put on the costume and cry, "Oh, this is just what I had imagined. It is perfect. I feel great. I can see the whole thing falling into place." Usually when the actor puts on his wig and costume for the first time, he needs tremendous reassurance and understanding. He needs help from both director and designer. First, the director must assure the actor that he looks good. "You look great. This is going to be wonderful." The actor doesn't think he looks great at all. The actor doesn't know how he looks. The director has to tell him in a loud, clear voice, "You look wonderful. With a few adjustments here and there you will look absolutely perfect." Within the actor at that moment two structures are teetering on the brink of collapse. One is his personal vanity. The other is his image of the role.

Secondly, the director must ask if the actor can move in the costume. Don't wait for the actor to complain that he feels restricted. You must say, "Can you move your arms freely? Can you raise your legs? Let me see you bend, sit, walk. Can you do that bit of business?"

Thirdly, the director must let the actor know that he is an ally in achieving adjustments in the costume. If there are any disagreements, the director must subtly take the part of the actor against the costume designer. It must never be the director and the designer against the actor. Ask the actor, "Would you be more comfortable if the hem were shorter? Can you work easily in these shoes? Is the cape going to be manageable? The collar isn't too tight, is it?" At the fitting a director becomes the actor's servant and must be prepared to satisfy his needs. If he really looks awful when you see him for the first time, you have to jump right in and say, "It's going to be all right. We'll fix this and change that and alter this . . . don't worry. I'm not going to let you walk on stage looking anything less than perfect. Don't worry about a thing." The first fitting is a moment of severe vulnerability for the actor. The skillful director is sensitive to the moment and showers the actor with help, assurance, and encouragement.

## DO YOU TAKE AN ACTOR'S PREJUDICES ABOUT HIS OWN LOOKS INTO ACCOUNT?

Many actors have spent years learning what is becoming to them. "I can't wear turtlenecks, my neck is too short." "I'm short-waisted—I look best in a princess line." "My hips are too wide—I need width in the shoulders." "I'm short—could I have heels and a vertical line?" It is helpful for directors and designers to discover these characteristics before the costume is designed. The actors, especially the women, always appreciate questions like, "Is there some color that looks particularly good on you?" Katharine Hepburn has always requested high, tight collars. Some will benefit from discreet padding. There are certain colors that women with red hair cannot wear; it is practical to listen to their preferences.

I love women in the theatre to look beautiful. Even if the role doesn't require it. I favor the tendency to dress and style their hair as becomingly as possible; for the men too. The actor appreciates the effort to make him look splendid. The audience wants to see heroes and goddesses. They see plenty of the commonplace in daily life. Even Caliban, Cyrano, Rigoletto, Quasimodo should look magnificently ugly. A good director is aware of all the little tricks that help to flatter an actor's appearance: shoulder pads, hip pads, bust pads, "banana shelves," waist cinctures, shoe lifts, Louis heels, V-necks, vertical patterns, dark, slimming colors. An actor will look taller in tights if they are of the same color as the shoes. A slight train on a woman's long dress will add height. Be careful to keep clutter away from the neck. Ask for high hairdos for shorter women; favor drawing hair away from the face so that the profile is not obscured and so that the full face may be seen clearly at a distance. The director works with the costume designer to assure that the costumes are designed to enhance the specific actor in the role. The actor must feel beautiful and appropriate. Some designers become more interested in the costume than in the appearance of the actor. I remember being present at an incident during a dress rehearsal of a production of *All's Well That*

*Ends Well*. A very famous director shouted, "The actress looks awful. Get a new dress." The designer, from the other side of the theatre, shouted back, "The dress looks awful. Get a new actress!"

## SPECIAL SCENES

Once the play has had several runthroughs and the time to enter the technical phase is getting close, the director frequently becomes aware of two or three spots in the performance that are not coming to life, or which have special mechanical problems. At this point, it is valuable to isolate these scenes; take them apart bit by bit and restructure them, suggesting new ideas—extravagant ideas—driving the actor's attention once again to the choice of the right objective. It may be necessary to work with some mechanical apparatus in order for the scene to be made playable. Special rehearsals are called to iron out the remaining difficulties before the production is taken onto the stage, where an entirely new set of challenges awaits.

## COSTUME PARADE

Some directors don't use this particular technique. It may be that the director has seen the costume in the fitting room and is completely satisfied. In my experience this is rarely the case.

I always have a costume parade before the first technical rehearsal. The designers, the fitter, the draper, the wigmaker, the stage manager, and I stand on the stage in full light and we look at each actor, in costume, one at a time. We review his costume completely. We make sure all the snaps are in the right place; that it's not too tight in the throat; that there are no gaps where his underwear shows; that the shoes fit; that the hat doesn't fall off; and that he can move his arms. "Let me see you do that little piece of business! Will it work all right?" You ask the actor to move around the furniture and up and down the stairs. You look at his wig under the lights to make sure that the join is invisible and that the hair style is flattering. In short, for a few moments you make a fuss over the actor in front of everyone.

The costume parade is an opportunity to discover whether we have overlooked anything inhibiting the actor's comfort. Here the actor is invited to give his final notes on his costume. "The wrists are too tight," "The boots squeak," "The petticoat slides down."

Another reason for having a costume parade is that you don't want the actor to give notes directly to the designer. Designers don't like it and occasionally retaliate by slighting the actor or even by insulting him. The actor gives his notes to the director. "This feels a little awkward, can you do something about it?" And the director turns to the designer and says, "Yes, he needs that to be loosened there." The director must be an arbiter between the designer and the actor.

At the end of the costume parade the actor should feel that his entire ensemble has been given attention, that notes have been taken, and that his costume will be delivered to him perfect, complete, comfortable, and ready for the performance. Giving this complete attention prevents future grumbling behind the scenes. It prevents the actor from feeling that nobody cares. A costume parade does take time away from the technical rehearsal, but it provides confidence and communication that will save time in the long run.

## DRY TECHNICAL

A *dry technical* is a meeting that is usually held in an office or around a table. At this meeting will be the stage managers, the lighting designer, the representatives of props and scenery, and the director.

The director will open the script at the first page and go from page to page with all the technical personnel. He will read aloud every cue in his script: the raising of the curtain, the music coming in, the lights rising, the telephone ringing, the door slamming, the flying of the scenery, the fading of the music. He will describe in detail the effect that he wishes to be produced. At this time the stage managers will confirm that all cues are indicated to happen at the exact moment requested by the director. Each department head will receive a description of what is to be expected. The director works his way patiently and systematically from the beginning to the end of the play, covering every cue in the book and giving a description of how it will happen. Occasionally difficulties will be discussed, but it's much more important for all the individuals who are effecting the cues to meet quietly away from the stage and discuss the cues in advance, so that everyone knows what is expected at any given moment.

It may not be possible at the first technical rehearsal to deliver all of the cues as expected, but it's important that everyone knows the ideal effect that is being sought. This dry technical or "talkthrough" saves a great deal of confusion when the time comes for the onstage technical rehearsal. It saves a lot of shouting back and forth from backstage to the house and prevents misunderstanding and loss of temper. The dry technical usually happens late at night so as not to conflict with the actors' rehearsal hours. It is a great advantage to the smoothness of the production. The director really owes this time to the staff.

## DRESSING ROOM ASSIGNMENT

The actor is particularly sensitive and is especially prone to size up his esteem in the eyes of the company members when the dressing room assignments are posted. Actors secretly compare: "Who has a better room, who is more important and better liked, and who gives the better performance?"

A clever director takes steps in advance to insure that the actors are not startled into irrational emotional crises as a result of the assignments.

When making the assignments, draw the stage manager, the assistant stage manager, and even the producer into the discussion well in advance. Seek the stage manager's recommendation. He will usually be objective and sensitive to the needs of the actors. Also, he appreciates being relied on for important decisions, and will surely think long and hard about the subject; since he will have to live with the actors once the play has opened, he will be strongly motivated to find a quiet, efficient, and agreeable arrangement.

The predominant factor in room assignment seems to be nearness to the stage, so that principal players, being busiest—rushing back and forth to touch up makeup, change costume, take a quick gulp of tea and honey, or make a swift repair to hair style—should probably be closest to the stage. The supernumeraries or chorus are farthest away, usually in the attic or basement. They must content themselves with sharing one large room and making do. Occasionally an actor who has a very swift change, or an older actor who is not good at running up or down stairs may be honored with the closest dressing room.

In the third week of rehearsal the stage manager prepares a rough listing of the assignments. The leading players who will occupy solo rooms are placed in order of priority. The featured and supporting players are grouped—women usually closer to the stage than men. After a discussion with the director, the stage manager may prepare an estimate of who will be comfortable together for a prolonged run—who shares the same interests, humor, tidiness, and so forth.

Remember that the moment at which the dressing room assignment is posted on the bulletin board is the same moment the actor is coming from the studio into the stage house for the first time. It is possibly a moment of great nervousness and insecurity. The actor feels the opening night performance looming before him like a raging lion. He is very sensitive. We do not want to give him even the slightest excuse for feeling betrayed. The reaction we hope to elicit from each actor when he reads the assignment is a sense of—

- Fairness: "Oh, that seems to be fair all around."
- Fulfilled Anticipation: "Looks, more or less, like what I expected."
- Delightful Surprise: "Hot dog! I get to room with my favorites, and I managed to escape having to share with so-and-so!"

• Self-Enhancement: "Seems I got a better room than I expected. Guess somebody up there likes my work."

When there is doubt about whether the actor will feel slighted at his assignment, it is best to call him aside *before* it is placed on the board in order to explain the situation and enlist his support.

## TECHNICAL REHEARSAL

Every director works a technical rehearsal in a different way. The following three descriptions represent the most frequently used methods.

**The Director-as-Star Approach**     Frequently one comes across a director who uses the technical rehearsal as an opportunity to be the center of attention. At any moment during the technical rehearsal he cries out in a booming voice, "Wait a minute, wait a minute." Then he takes his time while everyone watches him walk down the aisle, climb onto the stage, walk to the center, make a vaguely commanding sweep of his arm and say, "We have to have a solution for that." Then, standing with his hands on his forehead, he mutters an overlong "Aaaaah" while he thinks; then another prolonged "Aaaaah!" He kneads his brow, scratches his head and says, "Ah, well, maybe you could do . . . ah . . . ah, let's see, how should it be?" He spends a lot of time describing the problem that everyone can already perceive. Another "Ah!" Fragments of phrases—false starts at solutions—"What I want here is . . . Where are you supposed to be? . . . This has to be . . . Now the reason this doesn't work . . ." He moves in a circle looking at the floor with one arm extended as if he were halting traffic. In time he may patch a solution together, but until that moment he has simply been taking an opportunity to stand at the center of a crisis while everyone looks at him making up his mind; he tends to postpone the time of decision-making as long as possible. This style of work is his particular ego-payoff. He is aware that the whole production is waiting with bated breath for his decision. He enjoys holding everyone in suspense while his brain labors. Although this manner of directing is more popular than one might imagine, it reveals a person who lacks understanding of his office. A director is there to make things happen efficiently, swiftly, and deftly. To make himself a star at the expense of everyone's time, energy, and spirit is simple folly.

**The Start-Stop Approach**     Most directors use the start-stop technique, but it has very serious shortcomings. They begin the play at the beginning and as soon as something goes wrong they interrupt.

DIRECTOR: Stop that music cue!
 (One of the actresses snags her dress on the staircase.)
DIRECTOR: Let's have a look at the corner of that staircase!
 Is there a nail sticking out? Should we shorten her dress?
 Can you handle it, Alice?
 (Alice tries it again two or three times and succeeds.)
DIRECTOR: All right, let's start again from the beginning. House
 lights!
 (The action resumes.)
DIRECTOR: Where is the rain? It's too late. When she says, "It's
 coming down cats and dogs," it should be raining.
STAGE MANAGER: There's a lag-time in getting the rain machine working and we haven't timed it yet!
DIRECTOR: All right. Let's stop and fix it.

Some directors believe that the start-stop method is the only way. The difficulty is that this slogging from cue to cue takes a great deal of unnecessary time and is extremely frustrating to the actors and stage managers; but it is particularly exhausting and nerve-wracking for the director. The principal difficulty is that every time one stops, it takes four to six minutes to get started again. The following dialogue represents a typical effort to get started—any experienced director knows the following scene by heart.

DIRECTOR: There, now that we have the rain working, let's pick
 it up from . . .

ACTOR: I'll take it from, "You won't get away with this!"

STAGE MANAGER: Wait. That doesn't take it back far enough to give me my cue.

DIRECTOR: Well, give us a line then.

STAGE MANAGER: Take it from, "I don't have the letter, Alice."

ACTOR: (To Actress) Okay. Ask me for the letter.

ACTRESS: Wait till I get the gun.

ACTOR: You don't need the gun.

ACTRESS: Yes I do. I have to have the gun when I ask you for the letter.

DIRECTOR: What are we waiting for?

ACTOR: We need the gun.

ACTRESS: (Calling offstage) Jason, come back with the gun.

STAGE MANAGER: He's gone to his dressing room.

DIRECTOR: Couldn't we mime the gun?

STAGE MANAGER: (Offstage) Jason! Jason! (Long pause)

LIGHT DESIGNER: Are we going back?

DIRECTOR: Yes—to where she asks for the letter.

LIGHT DESIGNER: (Into intercom) Lights! We're going back.

ELECTRICIAN'S VOICE: But I haven't recorded this cue yet.

LIGHT DESIGNER: Never mind. Clear the board.

ELECTRICIAN'S VOICE: It's going to take a minute to get back into cue 37.

JASON: (Sticking his head in; he is half-dressed) Somebody call me?

ACTRESS: We're going back.

JASON: To my scene? We were timing my quick-change!

ACTRESS: We don't need you, just the gun.

STAGE MANAGER: You took it offstage with you.

JASON: It's on the prop table.

ASSISTANT STAGE MANAGER: (Offstage) I'll get it.

ACTOR: (Calling to director) Since we're going back that far, could we just do the bit where I crumple the letter and drop it in the waste basket?

DIRECTOR: What are we waiting for?

ASSISTANT STAGE MANAGER: Here's the gun.

DIRECTOR: Good. Ready?

LIGHT DESIGNER: Not yet. Lights are still setting up cue 37.

ACTOR: (Half-voice to stage manager) Could I have another letter?

STAGE MANAGER: Another letter?

ACTOR: This one is crumpled.

STAGE MANAGER: Oh. (Goes off)

ELECTRICIAN'S VOICE: Okay, we're back in 37.

DIRECTOR: Ready?

ACTOR: One second. He's getting me a fresh letter.

STAGE MANAGER: We don't have any more letters.

DIRECTOR: Couldn't we mime the letter for now.

ACTOR: Okay, what's my line?

STAGE MANAGER: "I don't have the letter, Alice!"

ACTOR: No, before that. When I crumple the letter.

STAGE MANAGER: "So much for blackmail!"

ACTOR: "So much for . . ."

STAGE MANAGER: Ready everyone?

ACTOR: (To Actress quietly) Could you give me that little re-action?

ACTRESS: What reaction?

ACTOR: Just before I crumple the letter.

ACTRESS: I don't know what you're talking about.

ACTOR: You know—you look toward the hall.

STAGE MANAGER: Ready?

ACTRESS: I can't look toward the hall unless I hear the door bell.

DIRECTOR: Take it from, "I don't have the letter, Alice!"

JASON: (Sticking his head in) We didn't time my quick-change!

DIRECTOR: Never mind. Never mind.

Does this seem like a parody? It happens all the time. As a matter of fact scenes very much like this one are reenacted again and again through the long and debilitating process of a start-stop technical rehearsal.

**The Barrel-on-Through Approach**   In our discussion of runthroughs we touched on the barrel-on-through approach; I will describe the steps I take to prepare to barrel through the technical rehearsal, and how barreling through can be turned into a creative experience for the actors.

1. I try to have all the sound cues—door bells, phones, clock chimes, dog barks, wind, thunder, automobiles, car doors, horns, crickets, frogs, birds—introduced by the stage manager on a tape deck during the working rehearsal—second week—or as soon as they can be prepared. This allows the stage manager some creativity to change and modify, to cue correctly, to estimate levels, to fade out and overlap. He becomes a player, and he takes pride in coordinating the sound with the scene so that a certain poetry of expression comes into play.

2. If there is a musical score, I try to have it completed on tape, with cues in proper sequence and with accurate leaders, ready to be added by the time each act is blocked—not later than the middle of the third week. At that time, I turn it over to the stage manager and again I ask him to become the poet. With his knowledge of the scene, he will bring the most appropriate timing to the coordination of action and music. I signal to him with the "go" cue and the "out" cue, as well as with any internal fade cues that I may anticipate. During the rehearsals I ask him to watch me closely while the music is playing. A gesture from me as we proceed will encourage him to start later, raise the level, fade sooner, support the dialogue, and so forth.

Stage managers love to work this way. It calls up the artistry in them. By working this way, we will have all the sound and music cues ready before the first runthrough. Having sound and music ready early has another advantage. It tends to push the actors a bit. They work harder and faster because they feel performance nudging them forward.

3. A series of meetings has taken place with the lighting designer:

A. A conceptual discussion takes place early on in which I describe in broad poetic terms the look we are after. I emphasize the colors I hope to see and the mode of the scene.

B. We go through the entire script a week before the first runthrough. I tell him in detail how I visualize each scene. I tell him where I expect practical cues and special effects, and I give him a rough description of how fast the lights change.

C. He sits beside me at the first runthrough in order to become familiar with the shape of the production. I talk to him quietly or slip notes to him. For his benefit, I sometimes describe out loud the movement of the light effects as the action is unfolding.

D. After he has prepared a light plot and I have reviewed it at home, we meet to place rough cues in his script. We give tentative numbers to cues and I describe what I expect for each setup.

E. Before technical rehearsal—sometimes, unfortunately, all through the night before the first tech—he and I sit in the darkened theatre, with a stage manager or an assistant wearing one or another of the costumes, or a facsimile of the same color, and the assistant walks the action while we set the cues. The cues set at such a time are always very rough. They seldom turn out to be right. One invariably has to change every one of them when the actors arrive on the set. But this first rough draft of lighting warms up the designer. It gets his fingers working. He sees how things work: where the backlight falls, where the spills occur, where the balances are, where the poetry is, where the surprises are, where the focuses need to be changed, where the gel is too bright or too heavy. He learns how the specials etch out the darkness, how the "practical" lamps can make the fireplace and sunset appear "motivated."

F. At the dry technical we review and renumber all his cues with the stage manager present. I estimate the number of seconds for each fade and we record the count with the stage manager.

So at the arrival of the first technical rehearsal, the lighting designer is ready to begin composing artfully with his instruments. He has a rough draft for every scene, and at least we are now confident that the actors will not be standing in the dark.

*4.* Now it becomes apparent that there was great value in having the costume parade. Even though it took a little time away from rehearsal, each actor is now confident that—

*A.* His costume fits and is workable, and that it suits the character and the action; or,

*B.* That notes have been taken on it and that someone cares. He will not mind going through the tech rehearsal in his T-shirt, if need be, as long as he knows the costume has been seen, tested, revised, and is in the process of being made perfect. He has tested the working parts—the flexibility of the boots, the bulk and sweep of the cape, the awkwardness of the hat, the tightness of the collar, the give in the crotch. The women have satisfied themselves that they will be attractive, that their skirts and petticoats are manageable, that their foundation garments let them breathe, that their pockets will hold their props, and that their jewels have strong fasteners. So here again the story is confidence in the physical reality of the production. The actor will be able to get through the technical without panic, mainly because the surprises are being systematically eliminated.

*5.* The principal actors are usually required to have photographs taken for press purposes before the opening. I try to schedule the photo session before the first technical. This presses the wig and makeup staff into readiness. If there are special makeup challenges, we discuss them several days before the photo call and test them on the day of the session. I allow the photos to proceed even if the wig and makeup are not exactly what we will eventually use in performance. The press photos are a kind of warm-up exercise to test the makeup and hairstyles. This usually leaves a few days to rethink and modify our choices, to purchase or make new hairpieces, to secure a darker or lighter makeup base, to redress the wig, to recast a rubber nose. By the time of the first technical, a refined makeup and hairstyle are ready for inspection.

6. By now we have previewed all physical aspects of the production except the sets and props. On the day of the technical rehearsals I begin by calling the entire cast on stage:

> Please become familiar now with the set, the furniture, the props. Move around on the stage. Go everywhere your character goes. Test the stairs. Test the escape stairs. Be sure you will feel secure and safe going up and down, even in the dark. Test the door knobs and the fasteners and make sure you know how hard you have to work to close the door and keep it closed. Test it outside. Test it inside. Make the set your own. Practice your entrances, your exits. Sit on the couch; does it sink? Arrange the pillows your way. See if your dress catches on the corners, on the rug, on the furniture. Touch everything you will have to touch in the play. Try the lamp fixtures, the light switches. See how they turn on and off. Test every prop: suitcases to be carried; bags of groceries to be emptied; knitting or crocheting to be worked or stowed; cocktails to be mixed and handed; flowers, plaster dolls to be handled; plates or martini glasses to be smashed; records to be unjacketed and played; hair curlers to be removed; and guns to be shot.

It is useful and quick to have everyone go exploring simultaneously. It imparts a spirit of fun and adventure to the cast, and each makes a demonstration of his success, which he hopes the director will notice.

Then we turn to the tricky bits—the pieces of stage business that may require special orchestration. We isolate them, giving our full attention to every detail, and to the comfort and security of the actors involved with tables to be set; dinners to be served; dishes to be washed; meals to be cooked; beds to be made; automobiles to be rolled in; dead bodies to be carried out; or disappearances, trap doors, and magic tricks to be executed. In addition we review the staging of any onstage dressing and undressing that is part of the action.

All aspects of the set and props have been tested at least once before we begin the technical rehearsal.

7. Now I call the actors together on the set. I ask them to

sit down and be comfortable while I speak to them. What I say may be something like this:

Now, my dear ones, we have arrived at the moment in which we draw everything together for the first time. You are used to the sound and music cues added in the early rehearsals, but now that we are on a new speaker system, some of the cues may be louder than we expect and they may come from places we didn't anticipate. We may have a few surprises, but try to absorb them and continue. The lights are in a state of "rough draft." We have *some* light for every scene but you will be confronted with incomplete cues, late cues, and so forth. Please be patient with us. We are working as fast as possible to make you radiant and beautiful. And please don't be distracted if you hear us talking in the house. We are taking notes and changing lights and working feverishly to make it right. Now it may happen that at some time you will find yourself standing in the dark. It is possible that the lighting designer is still working on a previous cue, or perhaps hasn't realized you are moving into that particular area. Please don't reblock yourselves just to get into the light, and don't drop out of character to ask, "Is this the light I'm going to have for this scene?" We will be working on it.

Most of the costumes are ready, and we have taken many notes during the costume parade of all that needs to be done to make your clothes completely comfortable and right. Remember during this runthrough (reinforcing the suggestion) that just as you are sensitive creative artists, the costumer and all the costume crew are sensitive and creative artists as well; so please don't stop and turn to me, throwing your hat or cape on the ground, exclaiming that you "can't work with this thing." If you have any difficulty whatever with a part of your costume, lay it aside and go on. We are watching you closely and we will take notes to remedy your difficulties.

For wigs and makeup, today is an experiment. I want to see the makeup you have designed and I want to see that the hairstyle is becoming to you under the lights. When I give you notes after tonight's runthrough, I will let you know where they need more attention. But if a mustache comes off, *don't stop.* Or if you lose your wig, just toss it on the chair and keep going. Don't lose the through-line of the scene.

Try to incorporate all the props effortlessly, without stopping. If there is a prop that you are unsure of, go now and test it; make it your own, so you won't have to stop to deal with it during the runthrough.

If you have any questions about how anything on the set works, ask now. Some pieces are incomplete. Some things won't be delivered until tomorrow. In these cases, fake it or mime it, but try not to interrupt the flow of a scene.

> What we are given is that with which we are creative. I know I can count on you.

After having enumerated the reasons why they should be confident in their abilities to deal with the unexpected, I break the gentle news:

> Now, my dear ones, even though a lot will probably go wrong this first time, I want you to *barrel on through!* If something goes awry, absorb it and continue. Even if you find yourself in the pitch dark, keep the action going. We will catch up with you. We are watching you, taking notes as fast as possible. I want this, rough though it may be, to be a runthrough *for you!* I want you to keep building on what you have structured so beautifully in the studio. Anything that goes awry will be remedied later. Be brave! Stay on top of it! Supersede difficulties! Make it work! Of course, if there is any danger to life or limb, I want you to stop instantly. Otherwise, let's just barrel on through and see what we've got.

Now the actor is, once again, required to push himself through an obstacle course. He expects to encounter many difficulties, but with a little generosity of spirit he will manage to get through. An actor loves to rise to the occasion.

The principal benefit of this approach is that it takes about one-quarter the time to get through the technical rehearsal. Secondly, the director, actors, and staff are spared the debilitating and discouraging plodding of a start-stop rehearsal. Thirdly, this press-on type of rehearsal requires the technical staff to witness the plight of the actors. This inspires them to find solutions to relieve the difficulties. Fourth, by forcing themselves to go through the obstacle course without stopping, the actors receive an adrenalin rush that will bring out more creativity. And, finally, the actors have the benefit of another complete, if somewhat lumpy, runthrough; and there can never be enough runthroughs at this stage of production.

## FIRST-TECH BLUES

In the passage dealing with memorization we talked about "off-book blues." Now we turn to something it took me fifteen years to learn.

The first technical rehearsal is always a disaster. It is always a complete and utter disaster. All the achievements and hopes built up in the rehearsal process collapse in an unrecognizable heap. The pieces don't fit together. Nothing is finished. Cues are missed. Lines are scrambled. Entrances are forgotten. The actors are befuddled. The props are late. The costumes look strange. The designers are disappointed. The crew is angry. The stage manager is dazed and the director feels lost—irretrievably lost. Yes, everything seems to fall apart, but it is *not the director's fault;* so don't give way to depression. And it is *no one else's fault,* so don't give way to anger. It happens. It is a custom.

Experienced directors anticipate the immense discouragement of first-tech blues. Each director expects one or more of the following feelings to career through his brain: "I'll never direct another play as long as I live!" "I wish I could disappear!" "What a hopeless mess!" "Where did I go wrong?" "I hate and despise the whole ugly thing!" "There's no hope!" "What am I doing here?" "I want to die!" Young directors should be forewarned that these are the standard thoughts that confront the stage director during and after the first technical rehearsal. No matter what preparations or precautions one may take, the first-tech blues are inescapable. Every director has his own technique for dealing with this phenomenon. After fifteen years of thinking I was the only director who experienced this problem, and that I was at fault for the disaster, I developed the following ritual:

Just before the technical I ask my assistant to run out and buy a jar of Skippy peanut butter, some Welch's grape jelly, a loaf of bread, and a container of very cold milk. The rehearsal proceeds, and even as I write a stream of notes like one long sentence, I slide down in my seat and slowly munch away on my consolation food.

This is the one moment that I really go for peanut butter and jelly, but the childhood ritual is a reassuring reminder that I am participating in another ritual that always has the characteristics of a bad dream. I willingly abandon all hope of seeing anything that even resembles what I had originally imagined.

At the first technical we expect to see everything at its worst. From this moment on, the production is gradually rebuilt until the moment when the play is ready to open.

## DRESS REHEARSAL

There is one principal characteristic of the dress rehearsal and that is that it is uninterrupted. It is absolutely essential that the actors be allowed to go from the beginning to the end of the play without stopping. The purpose of the uninterrupted dress rehearsal is to give the actors an opportunity to put all the pieces together and to rediscover the inner life of their characters from beginning to end. Any interruption would violate the actor's ability to slide into his inner life. At a dress rehearsal everyone connected with the production should endeavor to perform as if there were an audience watching.

It is my practice never to allow anyone to attend a dress rehearsal except the design staffs and those immediately responsible for the success of the production. There are no guests, producers, relatives, financial backers, baby-sitters, friends, agents, or students allowed in the theatre during a dress rehearsal. *If* there is more than one dress rehearsal, and *if* the actors are very comfortable working together, and *if* the production has had a smooth rehearsal period, I will occasionally make an exception to permit students or the public relations staff to observe, provided they arrive before the action has begun and remain in their seats until the rehearsal is complete.

## CURTAIN CALLS.

The staging of the curtain calls should be done only after the members of the cast have run through the play on stage several times and have become familiar with the scenery. It may well be done at the end of the dress rehearsal when the actors feel confident that the production is going to fall into place.

These are the characteristics of a good curtain call:

**Short**     Actors have a traditional expression: "Leave them wanting more." There is nothing more painful for an audience than to be forced to continue clapping when the spirit of their enthusiasm and their courtesy have been exhausted. Do it and get off.

**Crescendo**     If the entire cast is on stage at the beginning of the curtain call, there is no need for a crescendo. But if the players enter singly, in an order that corresponds to the increasing enthusiasm of the audience, it is desirable for the applause to build. It is also desirable to avoid a dip in the applause as it nears its climax. Artful staging can assure the curtain call of a "dipless" build.

**Characterless**     With the exception of curtain calls in which the entire cast stays in character—e.g., Feydeau comedies—it demonstrates very poor taste for one actor in the cast to remain in character for the curtain call while the others have dropped out of character. It is also important to inhibit the actors from sending personal messages to the audience during the curtain call. Spare us the exhausted artiste who has been so moved by his own performance that he can scarcely pull himself together for a smile; or the actor who sighs noticeably as he bows, rolling his eyes heavenward to assure the audience that he bears no responsibility for the shabbiness of the production. Some actors are tempted to draw special attention by doing little tricks like flipping their hat, or winking, or pointing to someone in the first row. These personal mannerisms should all be discouraged.

The curtain call must be disciplined ritual. The men should put their feet together, tight together—and the women too if they are not wearing long dresses. The actor should smile gracefully—even after performing in a tragedy. The actor should bow from the pelvis, not allowing his arms to loop forward to the floor as he bows; he should not grab his knees for support, but should let the arms rest gracefully at his side. The movements should be swift and undecorated. The curtain call is an opportunity for the audience to express itself. It is for the actor to retain a pleasant, uncommitted grace, acknowledging the praise of the audience with ritual gratitude. Keep it simple. Smile. Bow. And go away.

An important thing for a director to remember is that the actor is secretly evaluating his status at the time the curtain call is being staged. Here is the right order—the most usual and most safe—for a curtain call: The extras go on first. Then the small-part players may come on in groups. The featured players may follow in groups of twos and threes, and then the leading players. Now, when we get to principal players, we are in a most sensitive territory.

One procedure is to ask the principals to take their curtain calls in couples. Some plays lend themselves very well to this approach. For instance, the lovers take their calls together, as do the villains or the parents, then the principal performers take their curtain calls individually. This is an easy solution and usually the actors will consider it fair because frequently the lovers are balanced roles, as are the roles of the husband and wife, and so forth.

We get into difficulty, however, when we have a very good actor doing a brilliant turn in a small part, while a leading player who is carrying the play, working really hard, receives less enthusiastic applause. When possible, allow the script to be the determining factor. The size of the role in the script should dictate the actor's position in the lineup. The actors may be quite irrational and apprehensive as the staging of the curtain call commences: "Will I be called last? Do I get a solo call? Will the applause increase as I enter? Where I am placed in the order of the call will indicate whether the director thinks I'm any good. I'm better than so-and-so. He'd better not come before me. Will I be in the center of the lineup? Not on the side, I hope! Oh, disgrace! Well, at least it had better be fair to the character I'm playing!"

The director is aware that each actor has a great need to be reassured about the success of his performance. One of the most profoundly significant signals of approval from the director is the position he assigns the actor in the curtain call.

Let us now look at several plays for which the curtain call offers a special challenge.

***Romeo and Juliet*** Mercutio is always more popular with the audience than Romeo; and Juliet is *usually* a bit more popular than Romeo. If the trio enters in the order Mercutio, Romeo, Juliet, there will be an inevitable dip in the applause for Romeo. This will bruise the actor, so we allow Mercutio to enter alone and then bring the lovers on together. This way the applause will continue its crescendo.

***Othello*** There is an unspoken tradition of rivalry between the two actors who play Iago and Othello. It usually begins when the actor playing Othello perceives that Iago is getting laughs. Often, quite enigmatically, the audience cheers for Iago and is warmly polite to poor Othello. To avoid a dip in the applause on Othello's entrance for the curtain call, bring them on together. Later they may hand each other forward for solos, but by that time the audience has settled into routine clapping and they will be unlikely to favor either.

***The Three Sisters*** Here is a play with eleven principal players and each actor could deserve a solo call. One is usually trying to encourage the ensemble spirit in a Chekhov play, so that isolating the actors for star calls is a poor idea—someone is bound to be offended. One solution is to begin the call with the entire ensemble on stage and take all the bows as one group. Another possibility is to take the entire call in groups of twos or threes, with the three sisters coming together, arm in arm, at the end.

***The Man Who Came to Dinner*** This play poses a unique challenge. Whiteside is unquestionably the principal player and must have the final bow. But who should precede him—the four or five solid players with long roles who have been struggling through to hold the plot together, or Banjo, a relatively short role, a wacky one-liner who appears late in the last act, bringing the house down with a short bravura turn? Unfair as it may seem to the solid players, we place Banjo just before Whiteside in the call. The reason is this. His popularity with the audience will make an anticlimax for anyone who follows him except the star.

One must be extremely tactful in choreographing the curtain call, because if the actor feels betrayed he won't act well; he'll abandon his own performance. Sometimes one must resort to the use of magic tricks; sometimes you weave little patterns in order to make sure that the actor's ego receives satisfaction. If a director is kind to his actors and looks after their needs, he will never have to worry about egos *except* when staging the curtain calls and when assigning the dressing rooms. These are the occasions when an actor's ego is most sensitive.

## PREVIEWS

The custom of giving preview performances to audiences before the opening night is a recent one. In the "old days," a production was taken on the road and tested in other cities, sometimes for as long as ten to twelve weeks, until the play reached a taut performance level. In recent years, this practice has become so expensive that most plays are unable to go out of town, or to go anywhere for that matter, in order to work out the snags.

The practice of giving preview performances represents an agreement between the press and the management that a certain number of public performances will be given before the critics are invited. It is a very constructive practice. The more preview performances there are, the better for everyone. If it were possible to have six weeks of previews before opening night, there would be many more successful productions in the theatre; the actors would have an opportunity to refine, and the directors would have an opportunity to eliminate, troublesome spots and to heighten special moments. In most theatres these days, five or six previews are considered to be practicable. Ideally, each preview improves on the previous one, leading to the perfection of opening night.

## OPENING NIGHT

Between the time of the first rehearsal and the final curtain call on opening night, there is one period of time that is sacrosanct. Then "no spirit can walk abroad; . . . then no planets strike, no fairy takes, nor witch hath power to charm, so hallow'd and so gracious is the time."

The period of time of which I speak begins at the start of the final dress rehearsal and lasts through the curtain call after the opening night performance. Usually this period lasts approximately twenty-eight hours.

During this hallowed time the role of the director undergoes a marked change, although the change may not be noticeable to anyone involved in the production. The shift in the director's attitude is characterized as follows: The director introduces no new material and no changes in the performance. He understands that in the twenty-four hours prior to the opening the actor's mind and spirit should be untroubled and at peace. The actor should not be encumbered with having to deal with anything new. His confidence should be secure.

During this period the director is especially careful in everything he may say to each of the performers. The goal is to leave the production alone, without seeming to have deserted it. He must be in attendance, interested and caring, but he is no longer active in the process of fixing and patching.

If the actors are called for a rehearsal on the day of the opening performance, it is not because the director wants to change, add, or redo anything. I ask for a short rehearsal on the day of the opening for specific purposes: I don't want my actors wandering around all day with nothing to do. A short and very light runthrough of the first act will give them an opportunity to focus their day, exhaust excess energy, reduce nervousness, and get their motors running for the evening. When doing a comedy, there is a special advantage to running through the first act quickly and lightly.

In addition to this fragment of rehearsal, I spend considerable time repeating the curtain call—I rarely make any changes, but occasionally I'll remind them to smile, or to enter with their heads up, or to walk bravely. In giving such prolonged attention to the curtain call the cast infers the message, "He has run out of notes. Everything must be in perfect order if he can't think of anything to rehearse but the bows." Confidence is increased by the director's relaxed attitude.

Running through the already staged curtain call can never be taken very seriously by the actors. It gives my staff and me an opportunity to clap for them, which I continue to do no matter how many times we repeat the call. When the actors hear such prolonged clapping from us, the message is clear: "We must be good if he's willing to clap for us untiringly. We really must be okay."

Another important reason for calling a short rehearsal on the day of the opening is to give myself an opportunity to speak to all the artists after the work is done and before the critics and audiences take over. After running curtain calls, I ask the actors to sit down on the stage, in the stage light. I get on the stage with them and ask for their attention for about ten minutes. Two things happen while I am chatting with them—one overt and the other subtextual.

The subtextual part is this: Generally the actor is present on the lit stage only while he is acting. Now, for a change, he may sit quietly on the set with the lights burning down on him like so many suns. He may allow his eyes to wander through the darkened house—a luxury never permitted during the action of the play. He may unconsciously explore the artifice of the set or props while I am talking. In a sense he "makes himself at home" in an untroubled, unhurried atmosphere. He loves the warmth of the lights, and he experiences a sense of heightened well-being. So much for the subtext.

Overtly, what happens is this: I ask the stage managers to

make announcements—stage managers always have something to announce, and it helps to fill up the time. Then when everything is finished and there's no more to do or say, no more questions to be asked or answered, I talk to the cast quietly, simply, and sincerely. I never single out one actor or another for special attention, but address myself to them all as a group. I praise them for the quality of our achievement together. I tell them to "toss" the evening's performance, to play it once through lightly. I tell them I am honored to have worked with them, and I thank them for a very creative and enjoyable rehearsal period. Usually I allow my real love and gratitude to show for a moment and then send them off to prepare for the performance.

Expectations and nerves are traditionally high backstage at half-hour before the opening-night curtain. There are some directors who go rallying backstage, lavishing kisses and flowers and gifts and notes upon their actors: "Good luck. Break a leg. Isn't it exciting? Are you nervous? Don't forget this. Look out for that. Enunciate clearly. Pick up your cues. So and so is in the house. It's going to be a hit. Give it all you've got." This is all hype. It is contrary to supportive behavior. When the director goes backstage on opening night, his effort should be merely to check in and see that everything is following a routine path. "Is everything all right? Do you have everything you need?"

I visit each dressing room and repeat my phrase, "Once through lightly!" These words carry the message: "I am confident that you will succeed without effort. There is no need to be nervous or intense. Nothing is at stake. Don't try hard. Don't fret. Don't worry about critics. Have fun and toss the performance easily."

From experience I know that the opening night will be only as good as the average of all the previous runthroughs. At all costs, we want to prevent the actors from having an adrenal attack on opening night. This is why we play down the hype. We try to make the opening night seem ordinary.

# Connotations

## UNIFORMS, FLAGS, AND BANNERS

I once had the opportunity to meet the celebrated producer Cy Feuer, who, over the course of several decades, presented many distinguished works on Broadway. He related the following story about *Guys and Dolls,* the archetypical musical comedy, which opened under his auspices:

> When we opened *Guys and Dolls* out of town, the first act was two hours and ten minutes long. The following morning the director, the leading actors, and the designers all came together to discuss the first-act problem. In that early version of the text Nathan Detroit was called by another name and his costume was nondescript. The ingenue, Sarah Brown, was described at great length in the script as a rigid, sexually moralistic spinster. But she was not a member of the Salvation Army when we opened out of town. What we did to solve the problem was, we gave both of them uniforms.
>
> Mr. Feuer said it as if he expected a question.
>
> "Uniforms?" I queried.
>
> We gave Nathan Detroit a blue pin-striped suit, a white beaver hat with a black band, wing-tipped shoes, a navy blue shirt, a white tie, cuff links; we gave Sarah Brown the costume of the Salvation Army. Right away we were able to cut an hour and ten minutes of exposition out of the first act.

This little story had a profound effect on my training. Over the years the story evolved into a principle of directing that has been an aid to me at difficult times.

It took an hour and ten minutes to *describe* Nathan and Sarah, to recount their historical background, to develop opportunities for revealing his waywardness and her priggishness. But by placing uniforms on them, the need for all that dialogue was obviated. It is clear that there are visual symbols in our culture that tell a story without words. A skillful director will have a very creative eye for the possibility of revealing the story through the visual symbols and not relying on the words.

By following this idea to its illogical conclusion, I later played with an entire system of visual symbols. I classified them under the titles of "uniforms," "flags," and "banners."

**Uniforms**    The best illustration of a uniform is the one already given by Cy Feuer.

**Flags**    A flag represents a prop—something that is carried. For example, in *Porgy and Bess* it is essential to inform the audience at the start of the second scene that Bess has been living comfortably with Porgy for several months—she no longer wears the uniform of a street girl; she has abandoned her beaded red dress for a plain, pale blue housedress with an apron. But to drive the picturization into even greater clarity, we place in her hands the flag of a large ceramic bowl and a dish towel. Upon her entrance she is seen just finishing drying the dishes. The connotative story is complete; it is not necessary to add lines or program notes stating that Bess has been living contentedly with Porgy for some time.

**Banners**    Certain rituals in life happen in very rigid forms. For example: A judge usually sits at a slightly elevated desk looking down on everyone else in the courtroom while all the participants in court look up at him. A second example is a wedding, which usually has a symmetrical composition. The bride and groom stand or kneel together facing a preacher. The families are also usually grouped in a symmetrical arrangement. A third example is a cocktail party composed of many well-dressed people standing in a confined area, smoking, drinking, making small gestures and indistinguishable noises. We give the name banner to any staging that has a commonplace or universal connotation by its very composition.

Quite simply, a uniform is a costume, a flag is a prop, and a banner is a conventional arrangement of people. The value of uniforms, flags, and banners lies in the connotations added to the story-telling aspect of the drama. The playwright sometimes provides these connotative values:

> Varya in *The Cherry Orchard* marches through the house with a heavy ring of keys hanging from her belt. This is a flag that connotes her position as boss of the household. Her guardian comments that she "looks like a nun." This could mean that she is wearing a uniform that connotes her virginity, a severe moral attitude, and a secret spiritual nature.

> Captain Queeg in *The Caine Mutiny Court-Martial* brings two silver balls out of his pocket and rolls them nervously in his hand when he feels threatened. The steel balls are a flag connotative of his increased sense of paranoia.

> Masha in *The Three Sisters* wanders through the attic rooms hugging a pillow. The pillow is a flag connoting her longing to hold her beloved in her arms. This connotation is both realistic and poetically revealing.

> The arrangement of masked diplomats leaning on a long table in the ballet *The Green Table* represents an important meeting. But it is the green felt cloth on the table that serves as the banner connoting an international diplomatic discussion.

> In the third act of *Our Town*, a funeral takes place. As there is no scenery called for in the play, the playwright ingeniously calls for a cluster of black umbrellas. These serve as a banner to tell the story of the funeral. The poetry and

connotative character of this cluster of black umbrellas is both eloquent and significant.

The great final scene in Molière's *The Bourgeois Gentleman*—the *Mamamouchi* scene—takes place under a banner of Turkish royalty. The elaborate Eastern decor, with music and dance, provides the banner of exotic absurdity in which Jourdain is exposed as a fool.

The fact that Hamlet persists in wearing black—a uniform connotative of mourning—for three-quarters of the play is a strikingly powerful gesture on the playwright's part. Many directors seize the opportunity to reveal that Hamlet's process of thought has changed by the time he returns from England by replacing the black uniform with some attire that will connote freedom of thought and clarity of vision.

In *Waiting for Godot,* Vladimir and Estragon wear bowler hats, baggy pants with suspenders, and long shoes. These are uniforms that are connotative of lesser vaudevillian comics. The uniform itself explains and enhances all of their dialogue. Indeed, if the designer were to dress them in, let us say, fashionable tennis togs, most of the play might seem totally incomprehensible.

These few illustrations may serve to stimulate the imagination of a young director. He will realize the maximum storytelling value through his visual picture if he drives his imagination to find the most revelatory flags, banners, and uniforms in each of the scenes he has to direct. If it is true that one picture is worth a thousand words, it is also true that on stage a uniform, a flag, or a banner is worth a hundred lines of dialogue!

## CONNOTATIVE COLOR

We have given attention to the connotative value of certain objects and clothing. Now let us consider the connotative value of color.

There is a nonverbal language that operates universally in

Western civilization at the subconscious level. This is the language of color. There is no doubt that certain colors represent certain things. This is true according to tradition and common emotional response. Let us run rapidly through the color spectrum and list some of the possible connotations of specific colors.

RED
: Passion; anger; violence; blood; physicality; rage; aggression; sexuality; materialism; glamour; danger; excitement; fire; hate; lust; revenge.

BLUE
: Peace; calmness; compassion; serenity; loyalty; friendship; innocence; intelligence; eternity; emptiness; depression; sadness; vastness; coldness; austerity; sky; ocean; iceberg; water; night.

YELLOW
: Excitement; sun; warmth; day; cheer; children; drought; riches; buoyancy; expansiveness; happiness; spring; morning; caution; disease; cowardice.

GREEN
: Nature; growth; prosperity; freshness; delicacy; spring; youth; progress; Ireland; money; sickness; evil; envy; poison; snake; reptile; swamp.

ORANGE
: Vulgarity; vivacity; boldness; uniqueness; contrariness; clowns; artificiality; vitality; assertiveness; fire; pumpkins; harvest; autumn.

VIOLET
: Royalty; wisdom; age; power; penance; wealth; ritual; old women; security; religion; feyness; snobbery; femininity; gentility; effeminacy; isolation; loneliness.

BLACK
: Death; evil; blindness; darkness; secret; strength; mystery; coldness; formality; sobriety; stricture; puritanism; conservatism; officialdom; dignity; permanence; infinitude; fright; the unknown; the void; abyss; loss; sorrow; depression; absence; emptiness; sophistication.

BROWN
: Earth; mud; fertility; autumn; wood; richness; animality; leather; malleability; warmth; reliability; nature; dullness; unadventurousness; subservience; poverty.

WHITE    Birth; purity; innocence; virginity; holiness; goodness; ritual formality; cleanliness; antiseptic; light; ecstasy; enlightenment; clarity; old age; vulnerability; sophistication; winter; snow; clouds; bride; wedding; strength, knowledge; wisdom; peace; spirit.

GREY    Age; ashes; ghosts; softness; confusion; uncertainty; obedience; conformity; depression; decay; lack of motivation; lifelessness; drabness; ordinariness; conservativism; lack of ambition; clouds; fog; vagueness; bleakness; boredom; tedium; mechanization; militarism; institutionality; government.

GOLD    Wealth; splendor; heat; sun; lion; ancientness; preciousness; value; sensuality; the exotic; class; timelessness; ritual; ceremony; heaviness; riches; greed; power; corruption; idolatry; glamour.

SILVER    Coldness; swiftness; hardness; moon; "secondness"; machines; technology; shininess; chromium; futurism; impersonality; impenetrability; inanimateness; security, numbness; formality; enigma; dignity, stability; ice.

Now these connotations may all be seen as subjective. It is very likely that in the above listings you have found words that you feel may be inappropriate to their color category. Everyone's impression of the connotative color will vary slightly. Yet, it cannot be denied that there is a universal language of color that appeals to the majority of people in Western culture. For example, consider flaming red and baby pink; they are both red, but they have two tremendously different connotations.

It is frequently a good idea to reinforce the character in a play by dressing him in a supportively connotative color. This is usually helpful to the actor as well as the audience. The fastest way to tell the story of a whore is to put the woman in a red dress. The fastest way to reveal a woman in mourning is to wrap her in black. The fastest way to reveal a blushing bride is to deck her in white.

When we reinforce the character with connotative color we are upgrading the story-telling power of the play. Colors are almost codified in contemporary society. As an example: Almost everyone agrees that grey represents an old man. Who is there who would send up a storm of protest, crying, "Ah, but *for me*, grey is a passionate color, a demonstrative, wild, recklessly lively color." In our society we observe the conscious protest of many elderly folk who choose to wear yellow, lime green, coral, and periwinkle blue.

Another example using grey: If we are dressing the lovers Hal Carter and Madge in the play *Picnic,* by William Inge, we would do them a great disservice to dress them both in grey. These are two passionate young lovers on the brink of discovering each other. A more appropriately connotative use of color would be to dress the virgin in pale pink and white, suggesting innocence awakening to passion; and to dress the young man in a silk magenta shirt, faded blue Levis, and boots and a belt of leather, connotative of a young bull. This visual story would underscore the action of the play. The connotative colors describe and reinforce the evolution of the passion between them. The use of red, white, and blue as the major colors on these characters also provides the connotation of something American; the scene takes place at an Independence Day picnic. These red, white, and blue lovers on the Fourth of July in an American town are making a bid for a position as a prototype.

When we describe connotations, we are essentially dealing with clichés. It is important not to dismiss a cliché. A cliché has come into existence because a universal truism has been repeated so often that it has become commonplace. Even though a cliché may seem trite, it is also likely to be universal. If a director goes contrary to the connotation of color, he ought to be ready to defend his choice. Correct use of color can reinforce, underscore, and clarify the author's intent with striking precision. Connotative color is a secret language between the stage and the audience, and the knowledgeable director will use color to maximum story-telling advantage.

## INCIDENTAL MUSIC

A more appropriate name for incidental music may be connotative sound. There are some plays that require no music; in
fact, to add music to some plays would be a disservice.

Many plays, however, are enhanced by a discreet and appropriate use of music. The difficulty of using music lies in making
the appropriate selection.

Music can be of tremendous value in a period play. In a sev-
enteenth-century play, for instance, the sound of a harpsichord
weaving playfully through the action evokes the spirit of the
period. The harpsichord is thus connotative of the period and
awakens many images in the spectator's historical memory bank.

It is a great mistake to choose incidental music that is rec-
ognizable, music that everyone can hum. Familiar music drags
the imagination down a familiar path. That path may have many
memories and connotations that are not at all appropriate to the
play.

On some occasions, however, it may seem powerful or extremely amusing to play familiar music. For example, the sudden introduction of *The Stars and Stripes Forever* at the end
of a comedy may add an absurd, slightly bizarre comment. The
distorted strains of Mendelssohn's *Wedding March* sliding up
under a love scene would make a definite statement, but, as a
general rule, we try to avoid music that is familiar to the spectator, principally because it carries a collection of unwanted
connotations with it.

One example might be the *William Tell* Overture by Rossini.
Generations of Americans have come to identify the *William Tell*
Overture with the Lone Ranger, so that one could never use
this music for background without calling up all of one's childhood memories of the masked rider. Certainly in a farce situation, the *William Tell* Overture may be used for a comic point,
although the effect might seem a bit desperate.

There is one piece of music that used to be played on the
piano so frequently as accompaniment to the silent movies that
it will probably never lose its connotation in American culture:
Mozart's *Turkish March*.

In the choice of nonfamiliar music, one may play music on phonograph discs, or have it specially composed. In using discs one has to be very careful of fading in or fading out the music so that the effect doesn't seem to be stuck on to the production in a mechanical way.

The most important consideration for incidental music is that the music not seem strange or foreign to the production, but that it have a quality of support, of increasing the flow and harmony of the drama, of underscoring and enriching the material. When used by a deft director, sound and music can bring tears to the eyes of the spectator, or laughter to his heart. The timing is important, the instrumentation is important, the tempo is important; and it is important that the dramatic action is reinforced and supported by the music.

## BUDGET

My grandfather had an expression that I have used previously, and it appropriately describes the relationship of an artist to his money: "That which you are given is that with which you are creative."

So often the artist cries that he never has enough money to do what he has in mind. Just as there is never enough time for rehearsal, there is never enough money to acquire the best actors, the best set, the best costumes; there is never enough money for the machine, or the fly gallery, or the turntable, or the elevators, or the louvres. Lack of money is always a lament in the theatre, as it probably is in all the arts.

We take a more creative attitude in this matter, however. We do not complain of lack. When I am creative with a felt pen on the back of a menu, someone will give me a sketch pad and a set of pencils. When I am creative with my pencils on the sketch pad, I will be given a canvas and some oils. When I am creative with my canvas and oils, someone will give me a wall and some pigments and plaster. When I am creative with my murals, someone will give me an architectural complex to decorate. The creative artist uses what he is given. When we began, we used crepe paper, Scotch tape, coat hangers, safety pins, and paper plates. When we have made small magic, we will be given assignments to make large magic.

There is a strong possibility that it is not the best thing in the world to have unlimited money. A shortage of funds is one of the limitations that causes creativity. Just as a picture has a frame and that frame limits the expansiveness of the picture, so also a theatre production has a budget and that budget limits the expansiveness of the spectacle. This limitation is a creative limitation. It is related to the principle that necessity is the mother of invention. If we must put on the play and all we have is butcher's paper and coffee cans, then we shall find something creative to do with the butcher's paper and coffee cans. This creativity will inform and delight the spectators as much as if we had put the entire Taj Mahal on the stage.

For the director, one measure of success should be that he bring his production in *just slightly* under budget—at least *on* budget. Being master of his budget shows the director to be an individual who has self-respect and respect for his surroundings—a person who uses efficiently what is given; who is careful not to splash about with unworkable ideas, changing purpose at every turn and squandering the resources that have been provided.

Another reason for respecting the budget and coming in under the line is that producers have a tendency not to hire a director a second time if he goes over budget. A young director hopes for a lifetime of employment, which is difficult to achieve if no producer will hire him a second time.

"That which we are given is that with which we are creative!" This applies to time, it applies to money, it applies to people, it applies to the theatre building, it applies to the audience, and it applies to the budget. The test of an artist: Can he turn the odds and ends, the flotsam and jetsam, that nature has dropped in his lap into a miracle of coherent creative inspiration? The surprise and the magic come with the realization that he has made something astonishing out of something peculiar and commonplace.

## SUPERNUMERARIES

The poor supers! They have been called everything: the extras; the crowd; the gypsies; the mutes; the walk-ons; the hemp and homespun; the ragtaggle; and the madding throng. How does a creative director approach a production that involves supernumeraries?

Some directors ignore the supers in the hope that no one will notice them, or that they will go away. Some directors leave the supers standing upstage in a vague line, looking something like a disheveled graduation portrait or an unemployment line. These disoriented extras make half-hearted exhortations toward the principal players, sometimes rocking forward and leaning in from the pelvis to indicate involvement. Such spectacle is pitiful, but to hear their bits and fragments of dialogue is even more appalling.

Never begin by rehearsing the principals and the extras simultaneously. Prepare the principals alone and add the extras later. Allow the principal actors to achieve a performance level at which they are comfortable with their blocking and line memorization before introducing the extras—one doesn't want to have the extras sitting around evaluating the principal players, or making demonstrations of boredom while the cast is being creative.

In staging the extras, a valuable method proves to be the study of the old masters. These painters had a manner of grouping—of putting heads together—so that a large canvas could be viewed easily. The eye travels from one cluster of heads to another. Before embarking on the staging rehearsals for the extras, I usually hold an orientation session at which I teach them a playful technique, something I call, for want of a more accurate word, *associating*. This word is a vague tool used merely to indicate that the extras arrange themselves so that there is some physical association; some bodily contact with each other as they group themselves in these clusters. It is not surprising that a large group of supporting players, who come together for the first time as strangers, are reluctant to touch or stand close to each other. It is for the director to orient them in this regard.

160

In our preliminary orientation I create compositions by asking people to put their heads near each other and to touch each other in strange ways, resting elbows on knees, resting forearms on shoulders, putting arms around waists, leaning backs against thighs, creating unusual arrangements in which bodies overlap. This overlapping of bodies is what I call associating. We turn it into a game, so that when I call for a new composition the entire group will rearrange itself, each one jostling himself about until he has overlapped his body with two or three others, touching them in various and peculiar places, always arranging for their heads to be close together.

In our preliminary orientation I also describe the technique of *inner monologue* to the supers. The truth is that all actors talk to themselves while they are on stage. Principal players do it as matter of routine. The technique of inner monologue is not a strange or unusual tool for an experienced actor. Extras, however, are usually not experienced actors. Additionally, they are usually unfamiliar with the play and with their characters' attitudes. I describe to them the technique of inner monologue and then ask them all to create their own inner monologues during the course of the rehearsal time.

I also ask them to create very specific characters, and to give each of themselves a name, birthplace, profession, income, religion, politics, and personal history. The extras always appreciate the opportunity to create character, but they must be invited and encouraged to do it. In plays that require the extras to speak and to have reactions, such as the crowd in *Julius Caesar*, I do one of two things: Either I ask them to write down their own lines, which after reviewing I request they memorize and never change unless they have permission from me or the stage manager; or as an alternate technique, I assign lines to them as we go along, and ask them to write these in their scripts. I give them very specific things to say that will give flavor to the situation, as well as give them something to believe in—gradually each builds his own character.

If the extra can feel as though he is a character in the play and that he is contributing something to the believability, he will enjoy the work more and he will act better.

In no case, however, do I allow them to fall into the abysmal world of vague muttering—"Ra, arraugh, arraugh!" or "Rhubarb! Rhubarb!" or "Fancy that! Fancy that! Fancy that!" The difficulty with the "rhubarb-technique" is that crowd scenes are famous for their sudden and sublime silent moments.

A silent moment in the midst of a crowd scene strongly resembles the silent moment at a dinner party when suddenly the conversation comes to a dead stop and none of the guests fills the pause. One of Chekhov's characters describes such a moment poetically, "The Angel of silence has flown over us." These sublime silences can be wonderfully revealing when they are intentional in a naturalistic play, but when they occur in the midst of a crowd scene, they offer a particular opportunity for disaster. For some reason, which no one can explain, the silent moment in a crowd scene is always filled by Big George, whom no one really knows very well—he was just passing through and got drafted into the crowd. But Big George always manages to bellow some unique phrase at full volume at the precise moment of the sublime silence: "And a car-load of rhubarb to you too, sweetheart!"

I remember a performance of *Julius Caesar* in which one of those silences occurred as Caesar and his retinue passed among the crowd on the way to the Forum. Big George was right there on cue, and everyone in the theatre—and probably the author as well—heard him cry: "Caesar, kiss my baby!"

Everything a super says must be consonant with the drama, and each super must know exactly what he is to say before the dress rehearsal. He must be accustomed to saying the same thing in every rehearsal. And he must never be permitted to say anything that would not stand by itself if he were suddenly overheard in one of those sublime silences. Comments unrelated to the dramatic action should be absolutely forbidden: observations such as, "His performance is down tonight," or "Not a very big house tonight!" Everyone on stage is required to participate in the make-believe.

In some plays it is very helpful to give the extras an improvisation or two. It helps them to understand the world of the play and it gives them a strong sense of being part of the dramatic action.

Some time should be spent impressing upon the extras the discipline of remaining motionless while the principal players are speaking—this is of crucial importance when the crowds include children.

The director must sense the precise moment at which the principals are ready, and at that moment the well-prepared extras are added, thus providing new stimulus to the principal players—a new exhilaration, an intensification of motivation—and a feeling of excitement to the growth of the production.

At the dress rehearsal, a policy of "offstage checking" should be initiated so that the extras check each other's costumes, hair, and props before entering. Whereas the experienced players are used to checking themselves, extras have a habit of wandering on stage wearing their glasses, their wristwatches, or missing their hat or gloves.

When you are working with crowds, it's a good idea to block them very specifically. For example, "Kneel on your right knee on the second step," or "Lean over as far as you can pointing your staff to the top light." Never say, "Be a crowd!" or "Make crowd noises!" or "React, react!" or "Be interested! Mill about! Be intense!" These generalizations are not useful.

When costuming the supers it is well to remember the old adage, Put your extras in greys and browns. The advice is, in general, sound. The colors on the extras should never upstage the colors worn by the principal players. This happens frequently in operas and in productions in which there is no color control. Imagine the chagrin of the leading actress, a brunette in brown wool with black trim, when she discovers a blonde chorus member in ivory satin and rhinestones standing directly upstage of her.

The supernumeraries must always be costumed and choreographed to support the action. No extra should be so interesting as to be mistaken for a principal player. The members of the chorus or the supers should blend together to make one animated statement—not forty-two solo statements—*one* statement composed of forty-two lively units. We develop techniques for casting, staging, and costuming the supernumeraries that will help to enhance the drama with color, composition, and movement; and with believable acting in support of the principal players.

## APHORISMS ON COMEDY

It is very difficult to talk about comedy and it is particularly difficult to discuss how to direct comedy. We will satisfy ourselves by giving consideration to some time-honored aphorisms.

**Play the First Ten Minutes Straight.** There is a strong temptation when staging a comedy to start doing funny things right away. This is a mistake and must be avoided. The adage goes that the first ten minutes of any comedy or farce should be played straight. The dramatic situation should be allowed to develop believability. If there are a lot of laughs in the first ten minutes of a play, the audience is not being allowed to enter into a belief in the world of the play. When an audience laughs at superficial gags during the first ten minutes of a play, they rarely laugh much after that. The actors and the director together must make a complete commitment to the believability of the situation. Once the audience is involved and cares about the characters, then comedic material will begin to rise out of the interplay of character and situation.

**Keep the "Set-Up" Clean.** Most experienced comics will decline to deliver the punch line if the straight man has fumbled the set-up. One of the necessary components for the set-up is a "broad balanced base." The straight man setting up the gag must not muddy or confuse the components of the set-up. It is usually best for his position to be motionless, steady, balanced; he is not leaning over, off balance, or in motion. The straight man should have a squarely solid residence in his physical position.

Secondly, the words and intent of the set-up should be totally clear.

Thirdly, the set-up should be delivered with absolute assurance; there should be no hesitancy, fumbling, or searching for the words. The set-up for a gag should have a broad, balanced base, and a "clean hard edge." It should be clear and lacking in movement, in order best to serve the "payoff" or "tag."

**Don't Move on the Tag.** An experienced comic dies a thousand deaths when someone coughs as he is delivering the tag-line of a joke. A very skilled comic will even decline to deliver the tag-line if someone is in motion, or if the set-up was muffed, or if there is some imbalance on stage. In such cases the comic frequently modifies or even abandons the joke all together. If the comic himself fluffs even one word in the tag, he knows the joke is unsalvageable and the laughter will never materialize. He will usually abort the joke by skipping it or by dissolving into gobbledygook as a rescue.

**Play the Situation—Especially When in Doubt.** The director must have absolute and complete trust in the humor of the situation. The greatest humor is derived from realizing and intensifying the truth of the situation. Always play the situation, always enhance the situation, always drive the situation to its limit. If there is any doubt when you are introducing what you believe to be comic material into the scene, favor playing the situation first and the comic material second.

**No Laughter in Rehearsal.** It may be that various successful directors disagree with me on this point. But when I am directing a comedy, I never laugh at what the actors do during the rehearsal. Nor do I permit the stage managers, the actors waiting at the sides, or any visitors to laugh either. There is a very practical reason for this. In rehearsal, an actor is extremely sensitive to everything that happens in the room. If he does something very funny one day and the entire room falls out with laughter, he approaches the moment the next day with anticipation and nervousness. He tries to do the same piece of business or use the same inflection that he used the day before. He steps outside the drama for just a moment in an effort to remember what it was he did that was so amusing. He tries to imitate what everyone laughed at yesterday. He fails to realize that no one laughs the second time because the surprise is gone. When he gives his attention to the memory of what he did yesterday, his belief in the character disappears, with the result that he begins to indicate; he externalizes and does merely a cheap imitation of what he did so successfully the day before. Then he goes home, grumbling, "Why didn't they laugh when I did it the second time?" The next day he tries again, and if again there is no laughter, he might come to the director, saying, "What happened to that laugh? Why did I lose that laugh that was so wonderful the first day?"

Let us say that the director has allowed the other actors, the stage managers, and the guests to laugh ad libitum during rehearsal. Since they know the actor and find him an imaginative and capricious performer, they might honor him with their laughter almost as an inside joke. Now when the play opens, the audience may not laugh in the same friendly manner, and the actor will feel betrayed. "What," he says to the director, "have I done to lose so many laughs?"

It is clear that no actor is prepared to be laughed at in rehearsal. His performance is not shaped. He has not found the continuity that will give him a true belief in the situation. He has not yet achieved the inner life. To laugh at him before he has realized the full picture is a monumental disservice. It is a mistake to believe that you are encouraging an actor by laughing at him in rehearsal. The production is not ready to deal with laughter until after the dress rehearsal.

**Keep the Clatter Coming**     I believe it was George S. Kaufman who maintained that for a comedy to be successful there should be sound—relentless sound—for the entire length of the play. He repeatedly required the actors to make all the words butt up tightly one to another. If there were a pause of any kind,

Kaufman would thrust some noise into the silent space: a door would slam, a phone would ring, a cash register would clang; someone would knock at a door, slap on a table, stamp a foot, crumple a paper, shake a martini, ring a gong, fire a gun, beat a drum; or someone would cry, sigh, scream, sing, mumble, cheer, grunt, gasp, giggle, or groan. Great comedic director that he was, he realized the enormous value of the momentum gained by a relentlessly uninterrupted flow of words. And if the words had to be stopped, some other agency of sound would slap, bang, or clatter to keep the comedic rhythm cracking. Then, of course, on those few occasions when he introduced a moment of silence—for a double take or for a slow burn—the effect was like a train wreck.

**Gags Come in Threes.** The learning process is the subliminal structure for a great deal of comic material. Many jokes are structured on an idea, the reinforcement of the idea, and then the payoff. This is a three-part gag.

There are some jokes that can be exploited three different times. That is to say, the same material presented with additions or variations may get three separate laughs, the second being—ideally—funnier than the first, and the third being funnier than the second. It is important for a director not to attempt to push comic material into the fourth or fifth stages of development unless he is absolutely sure he knows what he is doing. Many gags will pay off a third time, but will die on the fourth time, and would inflict bodily harm on the fifth time. The exception to this of course is a running gag. Skill and experience in comedy will tell a director when to push a gag for a second or a third time.

**Running Gags.** In *Charley's Aunt* the following line is spoken five separate times: "I am Charley's Aunt from Brazil where the nuts come from." The first time it is a moderate laugh. The second time it is well received. The third time it is a killer. If the phrase is to be used a fourth time it should be introduced with a twist, i.e., upside down or inside out. For example, on the fourth delivery the text may be modified to read, "I'm Charley's *nut* from Brazil where the *ants* come from." The fifth development of the line should take into account the audience's expectation. This allows the gag to expand one step further. The set-up is, "Oh, and who are you?" The actor delivers only the word "I'm . . ." and then articulates the remaining words with his lips but without voice. His fan might describe the words in the air, even putting a visual exclamation point on the end of the phrase. The audience, being ahead of the gag, will anticipate it—some of them will even say the line out loud for the actor. The fifth payoff occurs by pushing the absurdity to its illogical conclusion. A running gag may be implicated to the fifth if the director is very clever. There is nothing more appalling than a fourth or fifth implication that falls dead.

There are a few running gags that can work as many as seven, eight, or nine times. I have found that the best way to work on running gags is to work backwards from the funniest to the least funny. It is important with a running gag that there never be a letdown. That is to say, as the running gag progresses, each time must be funnier than the time before.

**Oh, That's So Funny!**     Now let us list a group of phrases that a skilled director of comedy never uses. Then let us regard an alternate list of phrases that are more effective for good creative comedy work in rehearsal. An actor never wants to think directly that he is being funny. He never wants to admit that he is trying to be funny. So a director alienates himself from a skilled comedic actor if he uses phrases such as:

> "Oh, that's absolutely hilarious."
> "That's the funniest thing I've ever seen."
> "You were funnier today than you've ever been."
> "The thing that's funny about this is . . ."
> "This will have them rolling in the aisles."
> "Let me explain the joke in this situation."
> "If you do this it will be tremendously funny."
> "The audience is going to die if you do that."

To speak this way to an actor while directing a comedy is like causing something to die. Remember that a comic actor is like a man on the brink of the most beautiful love affair of his life. He cannot bear to have someone come along and "objectify the relationship." You see, in consideration of the actor—who will ultimately welcome laughter—it is important in rehearsal to conceal our laughter. It is important to dance lightly past our fascination with the comedic aspects. We give primary attention to the development of the truthful situation.

Now, if it is absolutely necessary to address the comic structure of some moment, a skilled director will use oblique language, avoiding the use of words such as "funny," "hilarious," "outrageous," "delightful," "clownlike," "wipe-out," and even the word "laugh." An actor does not want to hear, "If you do it this way, you'll get the laugh." The actor is living in the illusion of a kind of innocence. He gives the appearance of being disinterested in "laughs." To say that this is "the joke" or this is "the laugh" takes away the romance, the purity. It's a bit like the lover who says, "Was that good for you?" Here are some phrases that a director might use to avoid the heavy-handed approaches listed above:

> "We *may get a little response* if we do it this way."
> "Try doing such and such; it may *give us* something."
> "We *may get something* if we do it this way."
> "We may be *missing a chuckle on this bit.*"
> "I think there are two separate *tags* here."
> "If we do it this way, *there may be a smile in it.*"
> "*There's probably a payoff* there somewhere."

The reason for the director's reluctance to discuss comedy is respect. The true comic cannot bring the humor to life until the audience is there. All rehearsals up until that moment are focused on the actor's effort to create and enter the reality of the situation; if you direct his attention to what is funny, you are asking for results. Any director who openly and blatantly asks an actor for result-playing in the rehearsal period is offensive to an actor, and the director will be repaid with anger and resentment. He will also be repaid, unfortunately, with a distortion and exaggeration of the moment that he was hoping to make funny.

**Playing for Laughs.** There was never a director so skilled that he could squeeze laughs out of a raw turnip. We are dependent upon the situation. The success of the humor in any dramatic situation is based on the full realization of the situation. The director of comedy must be doggedly, fervently, fanatically interested in the full implications of the situation. Go for the situation and press it to its most intense and improbable conclusions and the comedy will rise from it as steam from a bowl of hot soup! The director who approaches the script with the intention of making it funny will be seen by the audience in the very way we see a spoiled child who leaps about, flops on the floor, stretches his eyes, pulls his lips, waves peculiar objects—one may feel impelled to slap him silly as an arrogant, insensitive, nonparticipating, egotistical boor, whose interest lies merely in capturing our attention with no intent to fulfill our needs.

We must never get caught trying to be funny! The truly skillful comedy director must appear to be disinterested in the laughter of the audience. If he is discovered to be in blatant and hungry pursuit of laughter, he loses his credentials; the game is over; the audience goes home frustrated and disappointed, filled with, of all things, self-contempt.

## BEWARE THE UNRESOLVED GESTALT

The best way for me to convey a picture of one of the recurring dilemmas in stage production is to recount a story from my own experience as a student actor.

O'Neill's *Ah, Wilderness!* was being presented in the Studio Theatre. Ellis Rabb was playing the father, Nat Miller. I was playing the role of Sid, the drunken uncle. For my big scene I entered from left near the proscenium. I walked toward the center of the stage. Somewhere in my path was a small table, which had on it a large glass ashtray. As I walked to the center of the stage I nudged the table. The ashtray fell and I kicked it.

At the center of the stage I played my scene with Ellis and we were, of course, remarkable in every way. The ashtray was on the floor behind me. We roared and howled and whistled and sighed and sang and belched and dreamed and lived and died through a thousand dramatic revelations. But the ashtray was on the floor behind me. The scene drew to its conclusion. As I made a grand circle around the dining table beating my imaginary drum, I wailed and howled. I kissed and careened. I bleated and burped and still the ashtray lay crystal cold and uncaring on the floor behind me. It came time for my exit. Booming my bass drum from down-right, I began my triumphal march across the stage to the down-left wings. In my path on the floor lay the menacing glass ashtray.

Now, I had completely forgotten that I had knocked the ashtray off its perch on my entrance. Step by step I moved toward the door, acting with enormous ferocity; and I sensed that with each step a tremendous wave of warning ballooned towards me from the audience. The ashtray lay there almost defiantly in my path. As I neared it, a hundred silent voices roared at me from the darkness, "Look out, you're going to . . ." And sure enough, I did. I kicked that poor old ashtray again, streaking it into the wings with a clang that rang out and echoed through the theatre, everyone knowing the sound, everyone expecting the sound, everyone having heard the sound a thousand times in their anticipation. The ashtray crashed against the offstage wall with such remorseless vengeance that all the spectators groaned. How the memories of youth weld themselves into our minds.

That abused ashtray taught me one lesson that I will never forget. In the concept of the gestalt there is revealed a longing in the individual to complete an act that has not been fulfilled. An ashtray that has been put out of its place longs to be put back in its place. According to the gestalt of the ashtray, there is no peace in the universe until its place has been recognized and restored. The point of this prolonged story is this: The director must learn to respect every audience member's sense of the gestalt; one thousand individuals may be giving all or part of their attention to an ashtray hoping for its "completion"—for the resolution of its harmony—never even seeing the scene that is being played.

Although I was unaware of it at the time, few members of the audience were watching my brilliant performance as Uncle Sid. The lines could barely be heard, because the ashtray on the floor was demanding answers from the spectator. "Who is going to *pick up* the ashtray?" "Is somebody going to *trip* on the ashtray?" "Is anyone going to *deal* with the ashtray?" "Does anyone *care* about the ashtray?" "Is the ashtray *there* for anyone?" The ashtray occupied an ever-increasing part of the consciousness of the spectator. I would never have been able to have the full attention of the spectator until the ashtray had been dealt with. It would have been better to stop the action and put the ashtray right, and then to continue with the revelation of the story.

If something is introduced into the production that causes the audience to become ill at ease, (1) they will not watch the play with the same commitment and involvement, (2) all the efforts of the actors to arrest the attention of the audience will be but moderately successful, and (3) the belief in the play will be retarded by the audience's distraction. The unresolved gestalt is holding the audience hostage in a sense of incompleteness.

Experienced actors know that if something goes wrong, "fix it before you continue." To continue while an unresolved gestalt hovers over the proceeding drama is frustrating for everyone! The audience cannot bear the suspense and the actors are wasting their time.

The ashtray is an example of a stage accident that introduces a state of imbalance. But the same state of imbalance is sometimes intentionally, and wrongfully, created by the director.

In the blocking plan for a production, it is astonishing how many directors are willing to create, or allow to happen, unresolved gestalts:

A prop from one scene is allowed to remain on stage through the following scene, in which the prop doesn't belong.

A fight sequence that is too unstructured gives the audience apprehension for the safety of the actors.

Water is spilled on the stage floor in one locale, and although the set changes two or three times, the puddle remains on the floor. Women in full-length skirts walk through the puddle, heedlessly dragging streaks of wetness hither and yon.

A couple of lovers, having a spat, throw pillows at each other. One pillow knocks over a lamp. One pillow bounces into the auditorium. As straightening the lamp is not part of the planned blocking or the timing, the lamp remains askew for the rest of the act. As for the pillow in the front row, the man on the aisle retrieves it and balances it on the edge of the apron, where it rests awkwardly until the final curtain.

A letter is torn up and tossed on the floor, and pieces of it remain there, even through the curtain call.

A plaster statuette is flung into the fireplace. The shattered pieces ricochet across the stage. The audience fears for its own eyes as well as the eyes of the actors. And then the audience spends the remainder of the act wondering which actor will unwittingly grind the white plaster into the oriental carpet.

A pistol is aimed at one character. The holder of the pistol announces that the gun is loaded. Then he points the pistol at the audience. If we believed him when he said it was loaded, we will suddenly believe that there is danger of the gun going off and hurting someone in the audience.

For the artists to continue acting a play in the presence of an unresolved gestalt is self-deception. There must be no time at which a danger to the truthful and believable evolution of the drama causes the audience to be so distracted that they are unable to listen. It must be acknowledged with great sadness that many directors are willing to ignore a wayward ashtray downstage-left while the actors are acting their hearts out upstage-right.

A director must control his production, never allowing the audience to experience a threat of danger to themselves or to the actors. He must not let the action appear so uncontrolled as to cause fear for the wreckage of the furniture or the set.

Controlled action and completed action: the stage events must never be so uncontrolled or so incomplete as to cause the audience apprehension, discomfort, or prolonged distraction. Sloppiness in this area completely disrupts the spectators' sense of belief—the very thing we are trying to strengthen.

# An Epilogue

## THE COURAGE TO ACT

Scientific studies in relation to art are always amusing if not illuminating. Here are a few scientific observations:

> An actor who plays Hamlet for two hours uses the same amount of energy as a steel worker uses in eight hours.

> Tests were applied to the nervous systems, hearts, skin, glands, and brains of actors before going on stage. They showed that an actor's "stage fright" is composed of precisely the same physical and nervous responses as experienced by a man confronted by a raging lion, or an angry mob intent on destroying him.

Which brings us to the matter of the fear of speaking in public. In tests taken to determine what was most feared by 2,543 American adults, the most frequent responses, by percentage, were as follows[1]:

| | | |
|---|---|---|
| 1. | Speaking in public | 40.6% |
| 2. | Height | 32.0 |
| 3. | Insects and reptiles | 22.1 |
| 4. | Financial problems | 22.0 |
| 5. | Deep water | 21.5 |
| 6. | Sickness | 18.8 |

| 7. | Death | 18.7 |
|----|-------|------|
| 8. | Flying | 18.3 |
| 9. | Loneliness | 13.6 |
| 10. | Dogs | 11.2 |
| 11. | Driving or riding in a car | 8.8 |
| 12. | Darkness | 7.9 |
| 13. | Elevators | 7.6 |
| 14. | Escalators | 4.8 |

It is astonishing to realize that the number who suffered from the fear of speaking in public was about twice as great as the number who fear death or serious illness. From people who are unused to appearing on stage, one frequently hears the expression, "I would rather die than have to go out there," or "It would kill me to get up and speak in public!"

Governments give medals to soldiers who rush into the jaws of death. An actor does not receive a medal. What reward could be so great for an actor to face such great fear? The reward may be that in overcoming his fear the actor feels a true sense of freedom and liberation while acting—the ultimate human experience, the joy of prolonged unity.

It takes great courage to act. One of the criteria that validates a professional director is a complete and loving understanding of the tremendous fear involved in acting. A director who realizes the palpability and harshness of this fear will speak to his actors with great respect and gentleness. His ever-constant goal will be to lessen the fear, to mollify the sense of panic, and to build a performance that will minimize the actor's apprehension of the moment when he must go before an audience.

An actor is a hero. All acting is praiseworthy if for no other reason than that the actor has the courage to walk from the wings to the center of the stage. For his entrance alone, he should be praised. Speaking takes more courage; and speaking in the person of another individual, with a commitment to a belief in that

---

[1] "What are Americans Afraid Of?" *The Bruskin Report* (New Brunswick, N.J.: R.H. Bruskin Associates, July 1973), p. 1.

individual's emotional life, is not only praiseworthy; it is *awesome*. Those of us who have the opportunity to assist the actor, by making his path more smooth, are honored to aid him; and we are grateful for the great gifts he bestows upon us—his creativity, his wit, his humanity, his suffering, his imagination, his energy, and his complete and perfect self.

## "GET LOST, TOTO!"

In a scene near the end of *The Wizard of Oz*, Dorothy, the Tin Man, the Scarecrow, and the Lion stand before the mighty image of Oz. The flashpots spew up phosphorescent flames. A globe glows with the face of an angry wizard. His voice thunders from the towers of the Emerald City.

Suddenly, Dorothy's dog, Toto, pulls aside the corner of a curtain to reveal good old Frank Morgan manipulating the levers that create the terrifying illusion. Seeing himself discovered, he bawls into the microphone; he raves, frets, and kicks at the dog in frustration. This is the picture of a director discovered in the process of practicing his art.

A well-directed play should seem effortless. It should seem to happen of its own volition. It should seem to happen as if it could not stop itself from happening.

A skilled director does not push. His fancy, his invention, and his imagination are not manipulative. In the final week before the dress rehearsal an artful director flutters branches across the sand to conceal his footprints.

The true magician of the stage responds as the Wizard of Oz responds when he sees the machinery of his magic-making exposed: "Pay no attention to that man behind the curtain!"

# Appendix

## ACTING TERMS AND TECHNIQUES

In the course of presenting some ideas about directing I have intentionally omitted discussion of acting technique. A conscientious director will have read every significant book written about acting. In classes and workshops, he will have tested each of these acting techniques and made them his own.

Any professional director can be expected to have not only an intellectual understanding of the following terms and techniques, but also a practical knowledge of when and how to apply them and what results they will produce.

| | |
|---|---|
| Biography | Personalization |
| Sense of place | Touching points |
| World of the play | Sense memory |
| Fourth wall | Emotional recall |
| Concentration | Effective memory |
| Focus | Mental movie |
| Objects | Image |
| Task | Magic if; "What if?" |
| Secondary activity | Trigger |
| Secondary point | Physical characterization |
| of concentration | Animal characterization |

Endowment
Substitution
Role model
Characteristics
Secret moment
Private moment
Inner monologue
Adjustment
Psychological gesture
Mannerism
Invisible envelope
Relaxation
Relationship
Given circumstances
Conditions
Indicating
Playing the objective
Super objective
Scene objective
Beat objective
Life wants
Motivation
Core; spine
Obstacles
Actions
Vulnerability
Communication
Truthful talking
Through-line

Instinct
Process; method
Impulse
Improvisation
Tempo; pace; rhythm
Upping the stakes
Upgrading the objective
Spontaneity
Feeling of the first time
Moment-to-moment
Imagination
Dynamics
Text
Operative words
Feature; point
Take
Double take
Slow burn
Running gag
Throw away
Pantomime
Mimicry
Inflection
Rhetoric
Scansion
English grammar
Pronunciation
Storytelling

# Biographical Note

William Ball founded the American Conservatory Theatre (A.C.T.) in 1965 and remains its general director. Beginning in the theatre as a designer, he turned to acting and appeared with regional companies and Shakespeare festivals across the country. He made his New York directorial debut with an Off-Broadway production of Chekhov's *Ivanov* which won the Obie and Vernon Rice Drama Desk Awards for 1958. He subsequently directed at Houston's Alley Theatre; San Francisco's Actor's Workshop; Washington, D.C.'s Arena Stage; San Diego's Old Globe Theatre; and staged several New York City Opera productions. His 1959 Off-Broadway production of *Under Milk Wood* won both the Lola D'Annunzio and the Outer Circle Critics' Awards, and in 1962 his *Six Characters in Search of an Author* proved another multiple-award winner and enjoyed an extended New York run. After directing at Canada's Stratford Festival, Mr. Ball returned to New York to write the libretto for an opera, *Natalya Petrovna*, with composer Lee Hoiby, based on *A Month in the Country*. In 1964 he directed *Tartuffe* and *Homage to Shakespeare* at Lincoln Center, and then traveled to London where he recreated his staging of *Six Characters*.

A native of New Rochelle and a graduate of Carnegie-Mellon University, Mr. Ball has been the recipient of a Fulbright scholarship, a Ford Foundation directorial grant, and an NBC–RCA director's fellowship. Among the first plays he directed for A.C.T. were *Tartuffe, Six Characters in Search of an Author, Under Milk Wood, Tiny Alice,* and *King Lear.* They were followed by *Twelfth Night, The American Dream, Hamlet, Oedipus Rex, The Three Sisters, The Tempest, Rosencrantz and Guildenstern are Dead, Caesar and Cleopatra, The Contractor, Cyrano de Bergerac, The Crucible, The Taming of the Shrew, The Cherry Orchard, Richard III, Jumpers, Equus, The Bourgeois Gentleman, The Winter's Tale,* and *Mass Appeal.*

He has directed three of his productions for PBS television, including *The Taming of the Shrew,* for which he was nominated by the Television Critics' Circle as best director of the year. In June 1979, Mr. Ball accepted the Antoinette Perry ("Tony") Award voted to A.C.T. for its outstanding work in repertory performance and advanced theatre training. In the same year, Carnegie-Mellon University presented him with an honorary degree as Doctor of Fine Arts. He is active as a teacher and director in A.C.T.'s conservatory training programs.